K. .ґ

Jan. 2007

MIND MATTERS

can we understand animal minds?

————— MIND MATTERS —————

series editor: Judith Hughes

(see back for further details)

———— MIND MATTERS ————

can we understand animal minds?

MICHAEL BAVIDGE and IAN GROUND

St. Martin's Press
New York

© Michael Bavidge and Ian Ground, 1994

All rights reserved. For information, write:
Scholarly and Reference Division,
St. Martin's Press, 175 Fifth Avenue,
New York, NY 10010

First published in the United States of America in 1994

Printed in Great Britain

ISBN 0-312-12424-4

Library of Congress Cataloging-in-Publication Data

Bavidge, Michael
    Can we understand animal minds? / Michael Bavidge and
    Ian Ground.
        p. cm.—(Mind matters)
    Includes index.
    ISBN 0-312-12424-4
    1. Animal psychology. I. Ground, Ian. II. Title. III. Series.
  QL785.B315 1994
  591.51—dc20   94-30259
                                                       CIP

contents

list of figures

foreword

'A philosophical problem has the form I don't know my way about,' said Wittgenstein. Those problems are not the ones where we need information, but those where we are lost for lack of adequate signposts and landmarks. Finding our way – making sense out of the current confusion and becoming able to map things both for ourselves and for others – is doing successful philosophy. This is not quite what the lady meant who told me when I was seven that I ought to have more philosophy, because philosophy was eating your cabbage and not making a fuss about it. But that lady *was* right to suggest that there were some useful skills here.

Philosophising then, is not just a form of highbrow chess for postgraduate students; it is becoming conscious of the shape of our lives, and anybody may need to do it. Our culture contains an ancient tradition which is rich in helpful ways of doing so, and in Europe they study that tradition at school. Here, that study is at present being squeezed out even from university courses. But that cannot stop us doing it if we want to. This series contains excellent guide-books for people who do want to, guide-books which are clear, but which are not superficial surveys. They are themselves pieces of real philosophy, directed at specific problems which are likely to concern all of us. Read them.

MARY MIDGLEY

acknowledgements

We would like to thank Jenny and Myra for their support, Judy Hughes for her editorial patience and Mary Midgley for her indefatigable sanity.

'Look how they drink,' Harry tells his grandchildren, lowering his voice as if in the presence of something sacred. 'Upside down. Their bills are scoops that work upside down.' And they stand marvelling, the four human beings, as if the space between farflung planets has been abolished, so different do these living things loom from themselves. The earth is many planets, that intersect only at moments. Even among themselves, slices of difference interpose, speaking the same language though they do, and lacking feathers, and all drinking right side up.

Rabbit at Rest, John Updike

1: the shared world

We are not alone in the world. But much of the time we give the impression that we think we are. Our cities, our science, our determination in shaping the natural world for human purposes; all these aspects of human dominance can lead us to overlook the fact that the world is shared.

Of course we know that there are animals other than ourselves on this earth. We eat millions of them every day. We wear bits of them. Many of us work and live with them. Some people work and live for them.

The sheer number of animals on the planet, like the number of stars in the universe or grains of sand on the beach, presents a problem to our imaginations. Even the number of animals slaughtered by human beings every day in this country is difficult to grasp. Still, whatever the scale of human consumption of animals, the numbers involved are small compared to the enormous population of the animal kingdom. Even the number of kinds of animals is enormous: 350,000 species of beetles have been named and classified. In a single kind of tropical tree 1,100 species of beetle have been found.[1] There are about 9,000 species of birds. And at least 3,000 species of mammals. In the South American rain forest there are estimated to be hundreds of kinds of monkey that are found nowhere else. In fact, we do not even know how many species we have recorded – estimates vary between 1.4 and 1.8 million. But current estimates of the total number are even more speculative, ranging from 3 million to more than 10 million. Given this degree of ignorance about the number of species, there is little point in even guessing at the number of individual creatures with whom we share the world.

We are by now used to flabbergasting statistics about the

1

universe. But we meet a problem of a different order when we try to come to terms with the range and with the diversity of the animal world. What is this new problem?

It is one thing to think about how much of the world there is. It is another to reflect upon how many and how various are the viewpoints upon it. The number of animals strains our mathematical imaginations. But the diversity of animal experience presents us with a different and deeper challenge. What we have to come to terms with is that there are so many ways of perceiving the world, emotionally responding to it, making sense of it – so many ways of living a life within it. The difficulty is to understand how there can be so many ways of experiencing the same world. When we have accumulated even a great deal of factual information about animals we have still to appreciate the full force of the idea that sentience is various. The natural world is rich in its diversity not only of skin and teeth, flesh and bone. It contains a cornucopia of minds.

Despite the fact of the diversity of mind, there are powerful motivations for not taking it seriously. To begin with, it has seemed plausible to many theorists to deny the very existence of minds, other than human minds. Secondly, even if we recognise that we do not stand alone in the world, there are barriers to understanding how there can be kinds of mind that are different from our own. These obstacles to taking the diversity of mind seriously have a number of sources. They have roots in the ordinary things that we are sometimes inclined to say about our relations with other animals when we give the matter some reflection. They have roots in the traditional preoccupations of philosophy. Finally, these motivations are sustained by dominant strands of thinking within the rigorous study of other animals – the animal sciences. In this book, we shall try to understand these views, how they differ and what they have in common. We shall be concerned with the problems that arise when we try to understand the diversity of animal minds and how we can overcome them.

what people say

When we give other animals any thought, we are sometimes inclined to think that we know or understand very little about animal minds. But we don't all agree about why this is. The following are the sorts of things we say:

'Of course I can't know what my cat is thinking. I don't even know what you're thinking.'

'How could we possibly know what it's like to be an octopus? We have nothing at all in common.'

'It's all very well saying that you can just see that the chimpanzee is happy. But "happiness" is a human idea. You shouldn't impose human ideas on other animals.'

'Perhaps I could know what a lion is thinking, but only if it could tell me. Unfortunately, I can't talk to lions.'

These are not just different reasons for thinking that we don't know or understand much about animal minds. They are different kinds of reason. Still, we may think, they support a common position. We don't take the fact of the diversity of minds seriously because, really, there is no point in even trying. We cannot understand anything about animal minds. Perhaps we can have the idea of other kinds of mind in the abstract but, for these sorts of reason, we cannot give this idea any meaning for ourselves.

In this book, we shall see that these popular views about understanding the minds of animals reach down into a range of philosophical traditions, theories and principles about metaphysics, the nature of knowledge, experience, language and mind. It is worth briefly exploring these connections here.

'Of course I can't know what my cat is thinking. I don't even know what you're thinking.'

One kind of reason for thinking that we can't know much about other animal minds is that we can't know much about any minds other than our own. I can never really know what is going on in someone else's head. I can see the expression on his face, and the movements he makes, but that's not really knowing what it's like to be him. So just as I can't really know what it is like to be Fred, I can't know what it is like to be Fido. This view derives from the thought that because I cannot have something else's experience, whether human or non-human, I cannot claim to know anything about experience other than my own. Philosophers call this the 'Problem of Other Minds'. As we shall see, this problem arises in relation to any mind. Each individual mind is an island, whether it be mine, a cat's or an octopus'. In chapter 3, we shall examine this kind of reason for thinking that we can know little about animal minds.

'How could we possibly know what it's like to be an octopus? We have nothing at all in common.'

Someone who says this believes that, though we humans can know a fair bit about each other's thoughts and feelings, we can know little about minds that are different from our own. Though we flatter ourselves that we are each unique, we have, in fact, a great deal in common. To a great extent, we share a common life and therefore common experiences. I can know what my fellow human beings are experiencing because I have had similar experiences myself. But we do not share a common life with non-human animals. They are different from us. Their experience is not like ours. And, for this reason, we can know little about it. The more remote the animal is from us, the worse the problem is.

The difficulty here is not that there is a barrier between one mind and any other, but that there is a barrier between types of mind; a species barrier. Each species mind is an island; humans, crocodiles, cats, so on. In chapter 4, we will look at this problem in detail.

'It's all very well saying that you can just see that the chimpanzee is happy. But "happiness" is a human idea. You shouldn't impose human ideas on other animals.'

According to this view, though we find it natural to say such things as 'the lion is bored', 'the blackbird is nervous', 'the pike is malevolent', these are only things that we – human beings – find it natural to say. 'Boredom', 'nervousness' and 'malevolence' are human ideas. That we find it natural to use such descriptions does not mean that this is how things really are with lions, blackbirds and pike.

This is the accusation of anthropomorphism, the charge of inappropriately thinking of what is not human in terms that apply only to humans. Originally the accusation was levelled at the way religious believers talked about their gods as if Olympus was populated by bad-tempered politicians, albeit super-powerful. The same charge that was once levelled at talk about a world allegedly above the human is now levelled at talk about a world allegedly below the human. For many people, anthropomorphism is the trap into which we inevitably fall when we claim to know anything about other animal minds. We shall argue that anthropomorphism is a much more complicated issue than is often thought. There are many different kinds of anthropomorphism. As we shall suggest, it is less of a trap, more of a labyrinth, through which we shall try to make our way in chapter 5.

'Perhaps I could know what a lion is thinking, but only if it could tell me. Unfortunately, I can't talk to lions.'
This is an expression of the view that we depend so much on language to communicate our thoughts and feelings to each other that without it we are all at sea. Our position with regard to other animals is just like our position with regard to a tribe whose language is entirely unknown to us. We can see that something is going on but we cannot tell, because we cannot be told, what it is. If we could speak to the animals, we could know what is in their minds.

This problem turns out be deeper and more intractable than it seems at first sight. Is it really the case that language, the highroad of communication between human beings, is the great barrier to communication between humans and non-humans? In chapter 6 we will follow through the implications of our dependence on language for the problems about animal minds.

So, for these very different reasons, we cannot take the diversity of mind in the world seriously. It may be a fact, but, as an idea, it is just bare bones, without any flesh.

what animal scientists say

We might expect that giving flesh to this idea would be a natural task for the sciences that investigate other animals. Scientific curiosity has always extended to the physiology of non-human animals. Since the 19th century, the same disciplined attention has been devoted to the study of animal behaviour. If it is worth studying the physiology and behaviour of animals, why not try to understand the experience of animals and get to grips with the idea of minds different from our own? There are many in the animal sciences who agree with this. In particular, some scientists who see their work as part of a discipline called Cognitive Ethology, think that this is the whole point of studying other animals. But this is a minority view. As we shall see, Cognitive

Ethology is a controversial approach.

Historically, the majority view in the animal sciences has been that we do not need to take the diversity of minds seriously. Some of the reasons offered by scientists echo the things we ordinarily say – we just can't understand anything about minds other than our own. We might find this surprising – isn't it the job of science to overcome barriers to understanding? The response of some scientists is to say that the job of science is to supply scientific knowledge, and what we cannot have is *scientific* knowledge of minds other than our own. This response will be an important theme throughout this book.

There are other animal scientists who also think that we should not take the diversity of other minds seriously, for the simple reason that there are no minds other than human minds. It is simply a mistake to believe that, in any real sense, human beings share the world with other kinds of experiencing, thinking beings. It is unscientific therefore to believe that the world contains a diversity of minds. Consequently, it is not an illusion to believe that we are alone in the world. This too is a controversial viewpoint. Others in the animal sciences hold quite the opposite view. This disagreement means that, as a whole, the animal sciences are ambivalent about the diversity of minds. We shall devote the next chapter to describing this disagreement in more detail.

what philosophers say

If we cannot have a scientific grasp on the idea of the diversity of mind, we might expect that at least clarifying and making sense of the idea would be a natural task for philosophy. Certainly, philosophers have always been fascinated by the fact of consciousness. However, they have generally been much less impressed by its diversity. The contrast between the conscious and the non-conscious has formed the heartland of philosophical inquiry, whereas the contrast between different sorts of consciousness have attracted relatively little attention.

Philosophers have been amazed by a world that contains granite and clouds – and also minds. Of course, it may be that our convenient division of the world into those things that, broadly speaking, are sentient and those things that, broadly speaking, are not (give or take a virus or two), is a serious misunderstanding of how things actually are in the world. It is just, if only just, possible to think that there might be some very different, perhaps more important ways of being something in the world. More important, that is, than being either something more or less like Mont Blanc or something more or less like a stand-up comedian. Maybe there is a way of being something which is different from both. Of course we haven't the slightest idea what this might be. But it still might be the case that what appears to us to be a fundamental division in the world is just how things seem to us. Perhaps to any conscious being, the distinction between conscious and non-conscious reality must appear absolutely fundamental. Maybe the fact we are inclined to regard sentience as a cosmically significant feature of the universe is ultimately just a case of 'they would say that, wouldn't they?'

Still, it is plausible to think that there really is no more dramatic contrast than that between the conscious and non-conscious. And furthermore, if the idea of having a choice made any sense, it is obvious that being conscious, in the sort of way in which we are conscious, is just about as good as being anything gets. It beats being a rock. Since it is also the way in which anything gets to be a philosopher, the fact of consciousness certainly looks as if it deserves its central place in philosophical inquiry.

One important consequence is that the main problems for philosophers have been: how the conscious and the non-conscious relate to each other and which side of the divide any particular thing is on. They have been much less concerned to think about the diversity that exists on one side of the barrier: the kinds of experience. It is, then, because of the importance we have accorded to the division between the conscious and the non-conscious that philosophical interest in the existence of consciousness has overshadowed interest in its diversity.

There have been two exceptions to this general tendency. In the Judaeo-Christian tradition, there is a personal God. As part of their everyday faith, believers are committed to the idea of a non-human conscious being. Theologians have felt obliged to interpret this belief, to explain what, if anything, it makes sense to say about such a God. They have struggled to portray a mind which is omniscient, infinite, outside space and time, and which maintains a caring concern for the world. The religious imagination of the Middle Ages extended still further: a myriad of angels occupy the space between God and man. To the modern mind the question 'how many angels can there be on the head of a pin?' is the example *par excellence* of an intellectually futile speculation. In fact, the thought experiments of 'angelology' were designed to illuminate the nature of minds other than our own. In theology then, it has not been possible to ignore the questions concerning the diversity of consciousness.

More recently, there have been non-theological motives for the study of non-human consciousness. Animal rights movements have forced on our attention the moral status of our relations with other animals. It is *via* these concerns that philosophers have become interested in those questions which are raised by the diversity of consciousness but which are not raised by the fact of consciousness alone.

However, the aim of books on our moral relations with animals is to expand the circle of our moral sympathies. While they invariably open with accounts of the nature of animal minds, this is designed to prepare the way for the moral argumentation to come. Sooner or later, at some level or other, they downplay the differences between the human and non-human types of experience. For many of these thinkers, what matters from a moral point of view is what animals have in common with us. We cannot morally ignore animals if they have the same characteristics which attract moral concern in the human case. Consequently, the influence of the animal rights movements has been ambivalent about the diversity of animal experience.

Apart from these exceptions, philosophers interested in the nature of mind have done philosophy almost as if there weren't any animals. Especially in this century, philosophers have developed sophisticated and perceptive accounts of the nature of mind, of experience and of the character of beliefs and concepts. But only rarely is it ever asked if these accounts would also make sense when applied to kinds of mind other than our own. We shall examine this problem in chapter 7.

There is, then, a startling contrast between the extent to which we share our world with diverse kinds of animal mind and the low level of philosophical interest shown in the nature of their experience. There is not another feature of the world as obvious, as extensive and as interesting, which has attracted so little attention. It really is extraordinary how the world can be chockablock with animals, the schools crammed with philosophers preoccupied by the nature of mind and yet the libraries so sparsely filled with philosophical works about the diversity of mind.

why we should take diversity seriously

Our ordinary reflections, science and philosophy seem to put obstacles in the way of taking the diversity of minds in the world seriously. Why, despite this, should it matter to us?

We may think we know why animal bodies matter to us. No hamburgers, no brogues, no Derby winners; more controversially, much slower medical progress. Of course the history of human culture would have been entirely different without non-human animals. The development of civilisation depended upon the use of animals for food and clothing, as beasts of burden and as means of transport. We can get an inkling of the extent of our practical dependence on the animal kingdom by considering our exploitation of a single species.

Consider the whale. As Heathcote Williams[2] pointed out, through the exploitation of the whale, we have acquired ambergris, antibiotics, baleen filaments, bath essence, bodices, bread, brooches, brooms, brushes, busks, buttons, cakes, calcium, candle wax, car-wax, cattle-feed, chess-pieces, cigarette-holders, cooking oil, cosmetics, crayons, cuff-links, detergents, drums, ear-rings, endocrinal hormones, engineering coolants, fertiliser, fish-bait, fishing rods, gelatine, glycerol, golf-bags, gussets, hair treatments, inks, insecticide, insulin, iodine, laces, lamps, leather, linoleum, liver oil, mah-jong counters, margarine, paint, parchment, pet foods, piano keys, pigments for artists, pipes, plasticiser, racket strings, riding-crops, rissoles, sausage, shoe-polish, skin-cream, soap, springs, stays, steaks, stews, stitches, stock-cubes, surgical trusses, sword hilts and scabbards, transmission system oil, typewriter springs, vitamins, and yamotami.

This is just one example of the extent to which we use animal bodies as physical resources. But why should the diversity of animal *experience* matter to us?

Even when our primary interest is in animal bodies as a physical resource, we cannot afford to ignore the nature of animal experience. The whaler must know how the Humpback will react to the presence of his ship. The farmer prefers contented cows. Even the abattoir worker needs to know how to avoid panicking the sheep he is about to slaughter. Where we exploit not just what animals are made of, but what they can do, we need to pay even more attention to the psychological capacities that they possess. The shepherd must know what the dog feels about sheep. The jockey has to understand what makes the horse feel nervous. The mahout needs to be sensitive to the mood of the elephant. So even from the most practical point of view, it matters to us that animals see, feel and think. We make use not only of their bodies but of their minds. In order to exploit animals in the various ways we do, we have to take into account the nature of the experience of animals which is not all one kind of thing. The more complex our use, the more sensitive we need to be to their distinctive ways of reacting to the world.

Despite the enormity of our exploitation of animal bodies and minds, our interest in the nature of their experience is not confined to making them more useful. In our ordinary domestic encounters with other animals, most of us, most of the time, are quite happy to say all kinds of things about the experience of animals without feeling in the least uncomfortable or foolish. We say that the dog thinks that the cat is in the tree or it wants us to take it for a walk. We say that the horse enjoyed the exercise or that it must be feeling ill. We watch wildlife programmes and listen to the narrator's description of the bear's curiosity or the ape's concern for its young or the Emperor Penguin in the Antarctic winds trying to keep warm. Our ordinary talk about animals generates curiosity. We wonder, why does the pigeon fly home? Does the greyhound enjoy the race? When we share the sofa with the cat we wonder what the cat makes of the music, or us. Such spontaneous curiosity comes naturally. We feel that it must motivate the systematic search for answers and provide the foundation for scientific study. This is why we are surprised by the equivocal attitude of the animal sciences to the diversity of animal minds. In these ordinary sorts of encounter with animals, in our ordinary talk and curiosity about them, we do take seriously the nature of animal minds and experience. We see their experience as something of interest in its own right.

The clash between our exploitation of animals and seeing their experience as of intrinsic interest inevitably gives rise to a different kind of reason for being interested in animal minds. To an increasing number of people the way in which we have used animals seems outrageously immoral. On all sides of this huge contemporary controversy appeals are made to the true character of animal experience. The reformers tend to stress the richness of animal experience and its similarity to our own. Conservatives are inclined to emphasise its poverty and to distance it from the human. What they agree about is that the qualities of animal experience are relevant to how we should treat them. At the present time, these moral concerns are the most important practical reason for taking these questions seriously.

So our interest in animal minds extends from the grossly economic, through natural curiosity to the purely ethical. But there is still another kind of reason to be considered. When we reflect upon both our natural curiosity and the possibility of a scientific study of animal minds, our curiosity is stimulated in new ways. We find ourselves asking new kinds of question. The diversity of animal minds comes to matter to us in unfamiliar ways. We can appreciate this if we imagine what it would be like to live in a world which we did not share with other sensitive creatures. What, apart from the material benefits we derive from animal bodies, would be missing from a world in which we were the only species?

the world unshared

Suppose that only humans experienced a world, and lived within it. Putting aside the physical impossibility, the material losses, putting aside as well the aesthetic impoverishment – the beauties of the natural world restricted to landscape, skies, vegetation – what would a world in which there were only human minds, be like?

Some people may feel that life in such a bleak environment would be hopelessly impoverished. A whole range of activities and relationships, pleasures and satisfactions would be closed to us. We would not be the objects of animals' fear, aggression or attachments. We could neither exploit nor co-operate with domesticated animals. We could not enjoy the company of pets, nor observe the relationships of animals among themselves. The only expressive sounds to disturb the silence would be human: no warning calls of birds or barking dogs. These would not be isolated deprivations; they would transform our experience of the world. It would seem merely the place we happen to be. A global hotel, a human theme park, a stage-set for human dramas rather than the world from which we come and of which we are. Everything would have value only from the function it has in human life. We could have no sense of the world as a deep system in which human needs and purposes jostle with those of other species.

Someone might object that there is no problem in imagining such a world. We already act as if we lived in it. Our present exploitation of the natural world scarcely takes into account the interests of other species. However, it is one thing to override the interests of other creatures; it is another to imagine a world in which there are not and never were, any other interests to override.

Without animals, it would not be just the real world that was impoverished. The world of our imagination too would suffer: bereft of animals that talk, huff and puff at houses, pretend to be our grandmothers, and from whom we learn that modest persistence defeats over-confident pace. Further, the way we talk about our moral lives would be very different. We could not describe each other as behaving like sharks, wolves, lions or lambs. We could not identify the aspects of human nature in the way we do now – the animal and the rational, the humane and the beastly, the higher and the lower. We could not think of the human condition as lying between the apes and the angels. If we could not compare and contrast ourselves with the animal kingdom, our views of human nature would have to be constructed along radically different lines.

Imagining an unshared world brings home to us another reason for taking seriously the diversity of animal minds. That diversity affects the most general ways in which we think about the world and our place within it. When we develop a lively sense of the world as shared, there is a Copernican shift in our view of the world. We are not unique. The human way of experiencing the world is only one way of experiencing it. Take for example human senses. Our perceptual experience is dominated by vision. The world is for us a three-dimensional place of middle-sized objects perceived *via* their coloured surfaces. This is not the world as revealed to the complex eye of the fly, or in the electric field of the eel, or on the sonar map of the bat.

One natural reaction when we are struck by these questions is to think that our ways of perceiving the world are the right ways and these others are alien deviations from it. We might think that our senses reveal the world as it really is, whereas non-human senses are designed by Nature as tools of survival. As if, for example, the naked human eye saw the world unveiled whereas animals with 'weird' senses were more or less remote from the world, like the soldier peering through his infra-red night-sight, or worse, the air-traffic controller reading the world from his radar screen, or worse still, the astronomer decoding the distant galaxy from numbers on computer print-outs.

These different modes of accessing the world cannot be thought of as impoverished or deviant versions of the human. Nor can the worlds that they reveal be thought of as partial or incomplete versions of the world we know. There may be many advantages in having the senses that we humans have (though even if they were disadvantageous, we might well prefer them). But we cannot count among these advantages, that only the human senses reveal everything about the world as it really is. No doubt the usefulness of a sense determines whether it will survive the process of natural selection. But evolutionary success is no guarantee that the perceptual system of any creature gives exclusive access to how the world really is.

The differences between human and non-human forms of experience extend beyond perception. We may think of ourselves as builders, fighters, discoverers, scholars. But this is not the only way for a bright and energetic species to be. The dolphin's way of life is not a lazier version of ours. The lion is not a butcher with no hobbies.

(Maybe the capacity for experience of the world in *anything* like the way that we experience the world is not the only, or even the best way of ensuring the selective success of a species. The adaptive strategies of insects are a source of wonder. But do these strategies include or presuppose having experience? Perhaps organised social insects have a way of being alive in the world which is a genuine alternative to our own. Being a creature capable of experience is only one way of making a living.)

We, too, have our own distinctive viewpoint. In reflecting on the diversity of animal minds, we come to recognise that even our ways of thinking about the world – on which we pride ourselves – are rooted in our species nature. The way that we divide the world into different categories of things, events and processes is a function, not only of how the world is, but also of our own concerns. But it is difficult to understand what aspects of our thought reflect how the world is and what aspects are projections of our own nature. Reflecting upon the diversity of animal minds can help us to discover which is which.

When we think of ourselves as the only minds that exist, we are encouraged to think of ourselves as spectators outside the natural world, to think of our minds as bare searchlights illuminating the world from outside. But when we realise that animals, which are part of Nature, are just as much minds as we are, then we understand more clearly that we are in the world. We have a place in Nature. Despite our enormous capacity for bad faith, it is necessary to learn to respect this truth. This, in the end, is why the philosophical problems surrounding animal minds, which are the concern of this book, must matter to us.

'understanding animal minds'

At the outset, we ought to be clear about what we mean by the question which forms the title of this book – 'Can we understand animal minds?' We ought to be clear, but in fact what this question means will only emerge fully as the argument of this book progresses. It is a necessary if frustrating feature of philosophical inquiry that the questions pursued are only completely articulated as the answers become available. However, we can arm ourselves in advance against the more obvious misunderstandings of what this question might mean.

'mind'

We shall often talk about animal 'minds'. The use of the term 'mind' should not be taken as the expression of some particular ideological view about the nature of psychological states. Rather it should be regarded merely as a shorthand for referring to that range of capacities, states and processes which constitute the living experience of a creature.

However, despite the trouble that 'mind' may cause, we do not apologise for using it. To use the term 'mind' is not to commit oneself to the existence of supernatural entities nor to unscientific or outdated views about the nature of experience. We must be able to refer to how things are for a creature: in the famous phrase of Thomas Nagel's, to *what it is like to be*[3] a bat or any other creature. It is true that 'mind' is not the name of a kind of thing. But we need to be able to refer to a creature's point of view on its world. This book is in part concerned with demonstrating that there is such a need.

'understanding'

Putting aside worries about mind for now, what would count as *understanding* the mind of an animal? How could we know when we had succeeded or failed? What would it enable us to do? What, without it, would we be unable to do?

First of all, if anyone thinks that the only way to understand what it is like to be a lion is to be a lion, then the only way for us to arrive at such understanding would be to *become* lions. But this must strike us as a logically insurmountable obstacle. It is to say that understanding lions is a destination that human beings could never reach (see Fig. 1.1).

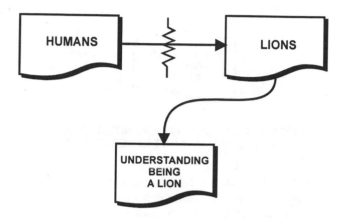

THERE IS NO SUCH THING AS OUR BEING LIONS

Fig. 1.1 Route 1 (A).

But even ignoring this problem, even if, *per impossibile*, we could become lions, a further hazard may prevent us from completing our journey. Many creatures, we may believe, perhaps including lions, do not have the intelligence to understand much about what it is like to be them. Many creatures have experiences of various kinds, but they lack the sort of insight into the nature of those experiences that we are seeking. The cat has near monochrome vision; but it does not *understand* what it is to have near monochrome vision. This may strike us as an instance of the general truth that it is one thing to be something or to have something. It is another to be able to describe it, comment or reflect upon it (see Fig. 1.2).

So, on this route, there is one insuperable obstacle followed by a hazard. This means that we must be careful that the standards for what would count as understanding animals minds make sense. In particular, we should not simply confuse *understanding* the mind of another animal with having the mind of another animal. To *have*

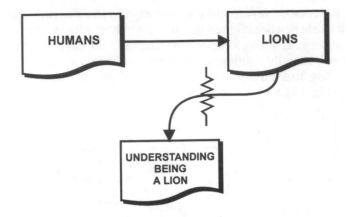

EVEN IF WE BECAME LIONS, WE MAY NOT UNDERSTAND BEING A LION BECAUSE LIONS MAY NOT UNDERSTAND BEING A LION

Fig. 1.2 Route 1 (B).

the mind of another animal in the relevant sense is simply to *be* that creature. So we must not confuse understanding a creature with being that creature. If there is to be understanding at all, we must preserve the distinction between who is understanding and who is being understood.

What this means is that there is no option but to take the direct route (see Fig. 1.3).

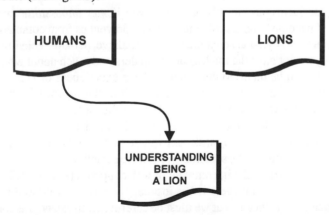

THE ONLY AVAILABLE ROUTE

Fig. 1.3 Route 2.

There may be hazards on this route too but, however formidable they may be, at least they are not hidden behind an insuperable obstacle. So what interests us must be the possibilities for *our* understanding of animal minds. If we conclude that no such understanding is possible, simply because it is our understanding, and that therefore the distinction between understanding something and being something collapses, then we ought to examine carefully our reasons for drawing such a paradoxical conclusion.

If *we* want to understand animal minds, it has to done from *here*, by us, by human beings.

species neutrality

In deciding what counts as understanding animal minds, there are some further considerations. We should be wary of laying down requirements that could only be met in the human case. We should seek to avoid approaches to understanding mind which, by definition, makes it possible to understand only human minds. As far as possible, and in the absence of any special arguments to the contrary, we should strive to produce accounts of mind which are *species-neutral.*

To insist on this is not to raise a moral objection to treating brute animals differently from human beings. Rather, it is a demand that what is represented on one side of the species barrier as conceptually impossible, is not, on the other side, represented as the best account currently available. While there can be excellent reasons why some philosophical arguments and positions must be species-specific, we must be sensitive to the danger of philosophy acquiring a degree of species-specificity which is quite at odds with its claims to generality and comprehensiveness.

So our standards for what would count as understanding need to be coherent and species-neutral.

objectives

This book has a number of objectives. They are all related to the subjective experience of non-human animals.

We believe that we need to overcome our reluctance to attribute psychological states and capacities to non-human animals, whether this reluctance arises from our unwillingness to impose human ways of thinking on the natural world or from the tendency of science to impose a single pattern on all knowledge. In particular, we want to encourage interactive and participative techniques in animal studies.

Within philosophy, we want to show that a particular psychological concept, the concept of expression, has been insufficiently exploited. It is a fruitful concept, a valuable element in an important philosophical task; the construction of a theory of mind which is not limited to our own case. For if there is a solution to the perennial problem of the relationship between mind and body, it cannot possibly be one that holds only in our own case. We need to develop a species-neutral theory of mind. But if this is not possible, the least we can be satisfied with is the recognition that our current conception of mind and its relation to the natural world, *both animate and inanimate*, is hopelessly flawed.

These ambitions are not original but are part of a sea-change in philosophical interest: from a preoccupation with objective certainty to a search for meaning and communication. At the most general level, we would like this book to help in removing the obstacles that stand in the way of a proper and rich sensitivity to the world as shared.

notes

---

1. According to a study quoted in 'How Many Species?', Robert May, in *The Fragile Environment – The Darwin College Lectures*, (eds) Laurie Friday and Ronald Laskey, (Cambridge University Press, 1989), pp. 61-81.

2. *Whale Nation*, Heathcote Williams (Jonathan Cape, 1988). A vast and beautifully illustrated poem charting our relations with the world's largest creatures.

3. 'What is it like to be a bat?' in *Mortal Questions*, Thomas Nagel (Cambridge University Press, Cambridge, 1979), pp. 165-81. Nagel is a contemporary American philosopher who writes about the difficulties of reconciling our subjective and objective views of the world. His question 'what is it like to be a...?' is proposed as a way of referring to the individual's subjective experience.

2: science and the diversity of mind

In this chapter, we shall give a brief historical survey of the main philosophical issues in the animal sciences. This is a problematic task. The history of any science is not simply a matter of logical progression, consolidation of agreement and accumulation of knowledge. It is also a matter of multiple perspectives, false starts and of complex misunderstandings. In addition, even to list the disciplines relevant to the animal sciences, from anatomy to zoology, let alone describe their history, is beyond the scope of this book. One way in which we can gain a perspective on the history of scientific investigation into animals over the last one-and-a-half centuries is in terms of the relationship between three sets of intertwining themes: evolutionary, psychological and scientific themes. While what follows is bound to be controversial, it never-theless represents something of the consensus amongst historians of the animal sciences.[1] If the reader wishes to dive straight into the philosophical issues, this historical survey could be kept until later.

natural selection
In the 19th century, animal science was dominated by the con-troversy over the meaning, limits and truth of the Theory of Natural Selection that had begun with the publication of *The Origin of Species* in 1859 by Charles Darwin (1809-82).

Darwin's explanation of the enormous diversity of life that we now witness contained two central claims: first, that evolution had taken place and second, that the primary mechanism of the evo-lutionary process was the natural selection of chance variations with greater adaptive value. The fact of evolution was widely accepted.

But the proposition that the Theory of Natural Selection was its explanation proved far more controversial. Indeed, it was not until the 1930s that natural selection established its dominant part in evolutionary theory and the animal sciences. As Darwin knew, a crucial weakness of his account was that the chance variations upon which natural selection was supposed to operate had to be assumed rather than explained. There was no account of the mechanism of heredity. It was not until relatively recently, with investigations into the gene and the discovery and description of DNA, that anything like an explanation of this mechanism and how it might produce variations became available. In Darwin's time, the absence of a convincing account of any mechanism of heredity made his theory vulnerable to criticism. In particular, it was vulnerable to the charge, based on the findings of 19th-century physics, that the earth was simply not old enough for the slow process of natural selection, operating on tiny and infrequent variations, to result in the complex natural world that we now see.

As it turned out, the geological evidence for the age of the earth, on which Darwin relied, was more reliable than the evidence on which the physicists relied. But, by the publication of *The Descent of Man* in 1871, this charge, among others, led Darwin to argue that evolution could proceed at a faster rate if natural selection worked in tandem with other evolutionary mechanisms. He brought to the fore his long-held view that habits, skills and novel types of behaviour acquired by parents, could be part of the biological inheritance of offspring – the view known as Lamarckism. What distinguished Darwin's views from those of Jean Lamarck (1744-1829) was that, for Darwin, evolution could not be thought of as a linear progression, purposefully moving from lesser to superior forms of life. Instead, it was a multi-faceted, pluralistic and value-free process; a tree with many branches, none of which could be thought of as better than others. In addition, Darwin argued that evolution occurred at a faster rate because of the mechanism of sexual selection. Animals can acquire characteristics which, while they have no direct adaptive advantage, nonetheless get passed on because they come to play a role in reproductive success. Exotic colouring, elaborate rituals, prowess in fighting conspecifics need have no particular adaptive advantage for a particular animal. Nonetheless, once such features come to play a role in the selection of mates, they acquire a selective momentum of their own. Supplementing the central principle of Natural Selection in these ways, Darwin hoped that criticisms about the rate of evolutionary change would be answered.

Darwin's development of his position left many contemporaries unconvinced. In particular, Alfred Wallace (1823-1913), who had independently discovered the principle of Natural Selection, thought that fundamental features of the human mind could simply not be explained as adaptive behaviour, produced by natural selection in the course of evolution or by the supplementary mechanisms posited by Darwin. He had been more impressed than Darwin by the abilities of the non-European peoples he had encountered while travelling and thought these abilities far beyond anything that could have been produced by selection in response to the demands of their environment. Hence, Wallace felt himself forced to posit some non-natural intervention in the original production of human minds and to insist that 'non-natural' cultural processes now drove our continued development.

Fuelled further by debate over the social and religious implications of Darwinism, all these themes came together in the great question of whether the difference between humans and other animals is one of kind or one only of degree – the question of our place in Nature. Either our development was a result of the process of evolution or it was not. But, for many in this great Victorian debate, if it was not, then our non-natural origin was clear evidence of our superiority over the rest of Nature. If it was, then it was equally clear that Nature must have aimed to produce us all along. So, either we were superior to Nature or we were its culmination. What could not be allowed was that we were just one product, amongst many, of a valueless and purposeless process; only one, attractive but not at all necessary, branch on the tree.

It is easy for us to feel superior to many of the protagonists in this 19th-century debate over evolution and natural selection. We can feel that they were childish and that we are grown up. Today, religious and secular believers alike, may think that we no longer feel the immature need to be at the centre of the cosmos and Nature; that our engrossments, our successes, our wonderful busyness, the subjective values and meanings of our lives, are perfectly fair compensation for our objective insignificance. It is part of the modern temper to be inured to our unimportance and contingency. It is part of the post-modern temper to revel in it. Despite such reactions, we should be wary of complacency.

The question of our proper place in Nature should continue to shape our response to the shared world.

animal associations

The same question emerged in subtle forms in another great theme that has dominated the animal sciences: whether the animal sciences must inevitably be about animal minds. This is the theme of our place in Nature written in the key of psychology.

Early in its history, the recognition of animal minds was a central assumption in the debate over the place of humans in nature. It had seemed to Darwin a consequence of the fact of evolution and the Theory of Natural Selection that the study of the human mind and the study of the minds of other animals were inseparable. Since we have minds, and there is a difference of degree and not of kind between us and other species, they too must have minds. For Darwin such a view was entirely consistent with believing that the evolution of mind, both human and animal, was explicable in terms of naturally occurring mechanisms.

This idea was implicit in the early accounts of the nature of mind. The dominating form of explanation in these accounts was psychological associationism. Psychological states or 'ideas' which, for whatever reason, occur in succession, are more likely to occur together again. The challenge was to show how this came about in a way that explained observed behaviour.

This kind of account seemed to have natural affinities with processes of combination that had been well observed in chemistry. Particularly important was the work of Alexander Bain (1818-1903) on the character of willed action – the 'instinctive germ of volition'. Influenced by the Utilitarian ethical theories of Bentham and Mill, Bain held that uncontrolled and spontaneous action became coherent and directed when the action became associated with emotions of pleasure and pain. The lamb could be guided by its desire to suckle only after its initially haphazard and aimless movements had, by chance, resulted in contact with its mother and her teat. Under the influence of the social theorist Herbert Spencer (1829-1903), this way of thinking about psychological processes became the 'Spencer–Bain principle': the frequency of a behavioural pattern is proportionate to the frequency of occasions when it has been followed by pleasurable events and inversely proportionate to the frequency of occasions when it has been followed by painful events.

This principle became enmeshed in the argument about the human place in Nature. Spencer, who originated the phrase 'the survival of the fittest', was zealous in the application of his interpretation of evolutionary theory to human society – in many ways prefiguring today's debates about the relevance of socio-biology – and where evolutionary theory went, associationism had to follow. Perhaps one day, psychological associationism might admit of a mechanistic explanation but, for the moment, pleasure and pain had to be thought of as psychological ingredients of both human and animal minds.

Insistence on the power of pleasure and pain to mould patterns of behaviour had always gone hand in hand with the view that the individual human mind began its existence as a blank slate, upon which experience could write its lessons in behaviour. In the case of animal minds, this supposition was modified by the work of Douglas Spalding (1840-77). Spalding showed that chicks deprived of early sensory stimulation were nonetheless later able to respond appropriately to visual and auditory stimuli – they could peck at insects and follow their mother in response to her calls. Spalding therefore distinguished between what was clearly and completely instinctive and what he named 'imperfect instincts' – patterns of behaviour which required some triggering experience, often during some critical period.

Spalding's work was important because it provided the first real empirical information for a debate that came to dominate the animal sciences – how to define the concept of instinct. For Spencer, instinct had to be understood as a chain of reflexes triggered automatically by external stimuli. But for others, the concept of instinct could not be separated from the concept of mind.

Romanes

Of particular importance in the discussion of the nature of mind was George Romanes (1848-94), who was widely regarded as Darwin's heir. Romanes held that the Spencerian notion of instinct was too simplistic to account for the complexity of the behaviour held to be instinctive. His *Animal Intelligence* of 1882 assembled a multitude of observations of animals from a vast range of informal sources to demonstrate that animals exhibited a wide variety of complex cognitive capacities. However, his accounts of these capacities relied heavily and, often uncritically, on the interpretation of the animal's behaviour given by his correspondents.

Romanes' ultimate ambition was to provide a classification of mental evolution to parallel that of physiological evolution. In a later work *Mental Evolution in Animals* (1884), he defended this general approach, presenting a full-blooded *dualist* theory of mind – mind and body are separate substances requiring different kinds of explanation. Nevertheless, Romanes argued, there is a bridge between the two. Intelligent behaviour, repeated often enough, becomes fixed into habits, and, embedded in physiology, allows the next generation to inherit the behavioural patterns. Still, dualist strictures remain in force. We can know that animals have minds, he argued, only in reasoning by analogy from our own case to theirs. For this reason, experimental methods would never be adequate to the task of understanding animal minds. Theoretical interpretation, based on our own case, of observations of animal behaviour in real situations was all that remained. We shall return in detail to Dualism and the Argument from Analogy in chapter 3.

Romanes' work and methodological outlook is crucial in the history of the animal sciences not because his views were accepted but because they were so widely rejected. For many, he is remembered only as a symbol of what the animal sciences must strive not to be. Indeed, it is arguable that the animal sciences acquired an image of themselves as sciences through the opposition to Romanes: their history is the gradual liberation of their investigations from the philosophical problems that troubled Romanes and would forever, it seemed, beset thinking about the nature of mind, both animal and human.

Increasingly, Romanesian themes in evolutionary theory, theory of mind and scientific methodology were all taken to be aspects of the same misunderstanding. These were:

- Lamarckism – the evolutionary thesis that acquired characteristics can be transmitted to progeney.

- Anthropomorphism – the inappropriate description of the non-human in human terms.

- Dualism – the philosophical thesis that minds and bodies are separate kinds of substance.

- Non-experimental methodologies – the use of informal or anecdotal evidence to support claims about animals.

Since these themes ran together, the opinion gathered force that they must be rejected together as well. If animals did have minds, then Dualism was the only available form of explanation. If dualistically conceived cognitive skills played a crucial role in adaptive behaviour, then Lamarckism was required to explain how mental evolution had occurred so rapidly. But if Dualism were true, and Lamarckism were required, then the animal sciences could never hope to be as objective and rigorous as the physical sciences.

Conversely, if the study of animals was ever to emulate the success of the physical sciences, both Dualism and Lamarckism had to be rejected. Consequently, so did talk about animal minds. In this way, the actual effect of Romanes' work was to encourage scientists to construct a reverse-image of his approach, in which to talk about animal minds at all was to put oneself outside respectable science. The theme of our place in Nature was transposed into the key of scientific methodology. This view was especially prevalent amongst those scientists, mostly American, whose primary motivation for the study of animal behaviour was the insights it might afford into human psychology.

Crucial in this coalescing of a governing form of methodology and explanation for the animal sciences was the work of Conwy Lloyd Morgan (1852-1936). Morgan formulated a seminal account of the nature of instinct as a causal mechanism built into the physiology of the organism. He argued that reflexes could be understood as relatively narrow responses of part of the organism whereas instincts involved the whole organism. With this distinction came the rejection of Lamarckism; a creature can inherit only physiology, reflexes and instincts, a capacity for forming associations between stimuli and the capacity for pleasure and pain. This rejection was further justified by the recognition that the estimate provided by physics of the age of the earth was likely to be inaccurate. (Ironically, it was the recognition that physics had failed to accurately estimate the age of the earth which aided the animal sciences in their ambition to become more like physics.) For Morgan, the methodological implications were clear and still today, for many animal scientists, the fundamental tenet of their investigations is the principle he articulated known as Morgan's Canon:

In no case may we interpret an action as the outcome of the exercise of a higher psychical faculty, if it can be interpreted as the outcome of the exercise of one which stands lower in the psychological scale.

This principle seems to be a version of Occam's razor, the principle of parsimony which claims that in explanations, entities should not be multiplied beyond necessity. Theories should be kept as simple and economical as possible. But Morgan presented this as a principle of evolutionary theory: if some simple process or mechanism is sufficient to produce adaptive behaviour, then there is no selective pressure to produce a more complex way of doing it. Not theory, but Nature, must be parsimonious. Morgan's Canon obviously raises the issue of what counts as 'higher' and 'lower' in the psychological scale and whether such a scale is compatible with Darwinian pluralism. But it also presented the possibility that the parsimony of Nature is the clearest evidence that we are not entangled within it.

The importance of these early debates in the animal sciences is that they set up a background of correspondences in terms of which the subsequent, much more sophisticated investigations were conducted. In particular, we can see in Morgan's Canon the formulation of a set of oppositions which came to dominate research into animal behaviour (see below). Moreover, Morgan's Canon came to be seen as enshrining the thought that the absence of any adequate account of mind must dictate the methodology of the animal sciences. For a whole tradition of animal scientists, anecdotal evidence stands to the scientific study of animals as introspection stands to the study of human psychology.

- Innate ⇔ Learned

- Inflexible ⇔ Flexible

- Non-experiential ⇔ Experiential

- Causal ⇔ Conscious

- Explicable through natural selection ⇔ Not explicable through natural selection

- Animal ⇔ Human

Behaviourism

From a philosophical point of view, the rejection of Romanes finally crystallised in America in the work of John B. Watson and the doctrine of Behaviourism. As Watson saw it, disputes over the subjective character of experience would run and run without resolution. If Dualism was the only serious theory of mind, then the only method available for the verification of such claims about mind was introspection, perhaps supplemented by anecdotal observations. In addition, Watson argued that investigation in psychology generally had not yet allowed the 'educator, the physician, the jurist and the business man to utilise our data in a practical way'. If the psychological investigation of ourselves and other animals was to take place in respectable experimental laboratories and if it was ever to lead to useful predictions and control of human behaviour, the solution was to eschew all talk about explicitly cognitive, affective and perceptual states. Instead, such states were to be understood as behavioural habits rooted in physiology and entirely explicable in evolutionary terms. In response to the objection that such an account of animals would be anti-Darwinian in separating humans from the rest of nature, Watson was not afraid to grasp the nettle. It was true that human beings were the only species capable of language. But what was crucial was to recognise that Behaviourism was able to capture this truth without the necessity to employ a distinctive vocabulary to describe it. 'The fundamental difference between man and animal...lies in the fact that the human being can form habits in the throat.'[2]

In a famous summary of the Behaviourist position, Watson wrote:

...one can assume either the presence or the absence of consciousness anywhere in the phylogenetic scale without affecting the problems of behaviour one jot or one tittle; and without influencing in any way the mode of experimental attack upon them.[3]

Ethology

However, the minimalist approach of Watson and his followers, eventually to include B.F. Skinner, was not the only one at work. In Europe, the majority of those involved in the study of animal behaviour had backgrounds, not in psychology, but in zoology. An important contributor to the European approach, which St Hilaire in 1859 called 'ethology', was the German aristocrat Jakob Johann von Uexküll (1864-1944).[4] Crucially, his philosophical background was not, like Romanes, the work of Descartes, nor like Bain and Spencer, the associationist views of the British Empiricists. Instead von Uexküll was fascinated by the connection between the theory of Darwin and the Critical Philosophy of Immanuel Kant. In particular, he insisted that the fundamental concepts in the understanding both of evolution and of the nature of animal experience must be time and, to a lesser extent, space. In *Theoretical Biology* (a title that would provoke derision from his later American counterparts), von Uexküll argued that the aim of investigation into animal behaviour was the specification of the animal's subjective world of experience – what he called the animal's *Umwelt*. The key to this was the investigation of the formal temporal and spatial features of the animal's experience. In exploring this idea, von Uexküll conducted a series of innovative experiments with creatures like trout and snails to determine the durations within which they could make sensory discriminations.

This kind of approach influenced some of the most important work to be carried out in the animal sciences. In 1973 Konrad Lorenz, Nikolaas Tinbergen and Karl von Frisch were awarded the Nobel prize for their work on 'the organisation and elicitation of individual and social behaviour patterns'. This distinction recognised their contribution to the development of ethology understood as the study of behaviour patterns characteristic of species and larger taxonomic orders; and giving special consideration to the evolutionary adaptations of behaviour patterns to the natural world.

Ethologists object to the almost exclusive attention paid by the behaviourist tradition within animal studies to processes of learning. As a result, ethologists tend to concentrate on unlearnt behaviour, particularly in the communicative interactions of animals which occur, for example, in display and aggression. They see communicative behaviour as social action which expresses a relationship between conspecifics.

In its attempt to develop a broad view of animal behaviour which takes into account the evolutionary history of the species and the animal's relationship to its fellows and to its environment, ethology sees the need for a pluralist methodology. Lorenz expressed his opposition to the 'truly ascetic and rather horrible sacrifices' that an ideological methodology demands:

> I find it hard to put myself in the place of a scientist who is ready
> to forgo the use of most of the cognitive mechanisms which
> normal man uses as sources of knowledge.[5]

Ethology relies heavily on the study of animals in their natural habitat. It encourages prolonged observation and detailed description, carried out sometimes over many years, rather than experiment under controlled conditions. The observations are often made as unobtrusively as possible to capture the animal's natural behaviour, though stimuli are also introduced to elicit responses.

Though ethology sees itself as a study of behaviour, it has in fact encouraged attempts to avoid thinking dichotomously about private conscious states as opposed to public performance. Lorenz declared that he 'wouldn't know where to draw the line between internal thought, which is not directly observable, and behaviour which is observable and is the result of that thinking'. Calling an action an attack or a threat or a conciliatory gesture is never just description of bare behaviour. Such words always include reference to what the animal takes its environment to be.

So the concerns and the methods of ethology are relevant to the themes of this book, in particular the emphasis on the life-style of animals, their social interactions and their relationship to their natural habitat as well as the hospitality it shows to a wide range of research methods.

The themes of evolutionary theory, the theory of mind and the scientific methodologies appropriate to the study of animals, continue to dominate the animal sciences. The present situation can be effectively illuminated by examining the contrasting views of two contemporary animal scientists who have made passionate contributions to the current debate.

two contrasting views

A recent representative of the Behaviourist strand of thinking is J.S. Kennedy. In a recent book *The New Anthropomorphism*,[6] Kennedy seeks to reassert the fundamental principles of Behaviourism in an attempt to forestall developments in Cognitive Ethology. He seeks to show that Cognitive Ethology is nothing but resurgent anthropomorphism.

Kennedy believes that whether or not a creature is conscious, or has a mind, or is the subject of psychological states, cannot be a scientific hypothesis. He believes this because he thinks such statements are simply unprovable, one way or the other. Therefore we cannot know that animals are conscious. Therefore any attempt to ascribe psychological states to other animals is both unwarranted and unscientific.

What then of our ordinary talk about animals? Why are so many of us so systematically wrong? Kennedy argues that our anthropomorphic talk, though systematically mistaken, is nonetheless natural to us and, in our ordinary lives, even useful. For Kennedy, the crucial distinction in his diagnosis is between the function and the cause of patterns of behaviour. The *function* (or evolutionary or ultimate cause) of a piece of behaviour is the role of that piece of behaviour in increasing the survival value of the creature. The *cause* (or proximate cause) is the causal mechanism which is now responsible for producing that piece of behaviour.

Thus, so long as we remember that we are talking at the functional level, we can say that the animals choose strong mates because they (or their genes) want strong cubs (or gene carriers). But this only makes sense because it is a shorthand way of referring to the process of natural selection. That is, we can use the term 'wants' because, through natural selection, Nature exhibits a kind of purposiveness. Natural selection operates *as if* Nature were seeking to maximise the adaptive values of species. Of course this teleological talk is itself metaphorical. Nature is not, in reality, an entity with purposes in mind.

However, Kennedy believes that anthropomorphism is acceptable when talking about ultimate causes, because it is intellectually profitable to think of natural selection *as if* it were following a rationally chosen means to an end. This is 'mock anthropomorphism'. So, talking about Nature as if it were purposive is just as natural and, so long as it is not misunderstood, as harmless, as talking about the way in which physical objects 'obey' natural laws.

What is not harmless is to describe functions as if they were causes. The animal may choose a strong mate because it wants strong cubs but that is not to say that the animal's present behaviour of mating with a particular conspecific is caused by *its desire* to have strong cubs. Again being sexually aggressive may serve the function of increasing the survival value of a creature. But a particular creature's present sexually aggressive behaviour is not (proximately) caused by its sexual aggression.

Kennedy believes that anthropomorphism has the special effect of making us likely to describe functions as if they were proximate causes. The ultimate cause of a piece of behaviour is transformed into a proximate cause and thus into a purpose which the animal is now pursuing. By talking of ultimate causes but thinking of proximate causes, we project the (as if) purposiveness of natural selection onto the inner life of the animal. And this in turn means that we think of the proximate causes as being psychological.

The alleged steps in the misattribution of consciousness to animals are then as follows:

•We treat ultimate causes as proximate causes;

• We project the purposiveness of natural selection working through ultimate causes into the proximate causes of a piece of behaviour in a particular animal;

• We conclude that the animal behaves as it does because its behaviour is caused by its purposes;

• We infer that since animals have purposes, they must have conscious awareness (of mental images of the intended action or state of affairs).

But if this is what is going on when we are being anthropomorphic, why are we so prone to do it? Kennedy argues that since the behaviour of animals is 'guided' by the 'purposes' of natural selection, animals often do behave *as if* they really did have purposes and so minds. Consequently, if predictions concerning animal behaviour are made on the assumption that they have minds, those predictions will often turn out to be correct. Since natural selection favours human genes which will allow us to be relatively successful in predicting the behaviour of other animals, human beings are naturally disposed to anthropomorphism.

So, Kennedy's view is that, in the animal sciences, we should only:

• identify functions of animal behaviour produced by natural selection;

- search for the actual mechanisms of individual animal behaviour which are the proximate causes that have been brought about by the ultimate causes of natural selection.

Mock-anthropomorphism is of use since it enables us to identify those functions which the proximate causes of behaviour must serve. Full-blooded anthropomorphism, however, prevents science from uncovering the causal mechanisms of animal behaviour by distracting us with psychological proximate causes whose existence and nature cannot be scientifically verified. At the end of his book, Kennedy takes these arguments to a dramatic conclusion:

> If scientists, at least, finally cease to make the conscious or unconscious assumption that animals have minds, then the consequences can be expected to go beyond the boundaries of the study of animal behaviour. If the age-old mind-body problem comes to be considered as an exclusively human one, instead of indefinitely extended through the animal kingdom, then that problem too will have been brought nearer a solution.

Griffin

Diametrically opposed to this are the views of Donald Griffin. He holds that the behaviouristic paradigm has been dominant for too long. He believes that it is stultifying the growth of the animal sciences, censoring useful observations and inhibiting the development of innovative empirical investigation. As he writes:

> Behaviorism should be abandoned not so much because it belittles the value of living animals, but because it leads us to a seriously incomplete and hence misleading picture of reality.[7]

In contrast, Griffin suggests that all kinds of animal behaviour require the use of psychological concepts for their explanation: from the chimpanzees' use of probes to gather termites and the beavers' building of dams and burrows through prey selection by wagtails, the predator monitoring of Thompson's gazelles and the self-concealment of grizzly bears, to the display rituals of fiddler crabs and the communicative dances of honeybees. Indeed, taking the argument into the enemy's camp, Griffin proposes what amounts to a denial of Morgan's Canon. It is simply not the case, he suggests, that causal mechanistic explanations of animal behaviour are always more parsimonious than explanations in terms of the exercise of cognitive capacities:

> ...to account for the flexibility with which many animals adapt their behaviour to changing circumstances would require an enormous number of specific instructions to provide for all likely contingencies. If, on the other hand, an animal thinks about its needs and desires, and about the probable results of alternative actions, fewer and more general instructions are sufficient. Animals with relatively small brains may thus have greater need for simple conscious thinking than those endowed with a kilogram or more of gray matter.[8]

So, Griffin suggests, the complex behaviour of leaf-cutter ants, with their tiny central nervous systems, is more readily explained by positing that their DNA enables the ant to have thoughts like 'Nibble away bits of fungus that do not smell right' rather than that it specifies the myriad complex movements and feedback systems required to carry out the activity.

This is, from the point of view of received wisdom in the animal sciences, a radical heresy: it suggests that conscious experience might itself be the result of selective pressure. As we shall see in chapter 5, there are severe philosophical problems with this kind of attempt to characterise the content of animal thought. But whatever we think of its truth, it does identify a crucial weakness in the behaviourist paradigm. If it is true that we can find out all there is to know about animals and ourselves without the use of psychological concepts, then we are left with the question: what is (our) experience for? Why has Nature bothered with it? It is possible that we are wrong about the nature of our experience. But could we really be wrong in thinking that experience is of any importance to the *natural* life of human beings at all?

Griffin is, of course, sensitive to the accusation that, in the past, study of the conscious experience of animals has not proved empirically productive. He, therefore, is keen to suggest a variety of ways in which this cognitive approach may be experimentally fruitful. Some of these techniques are tentative suggestions concerning the monitoring of neurophysiological electrical activity and correlations with conscious thinking in humans. But Griffin places by far the greatest emphasis on close observation of, and interaction with animals in the wild. In particular, he emphasises the role of *interactive methodologies* in which the source of data about the animal is communication between the animal and the scientist. The researcher can take part in communication either directly – as occurs in many studies of apes – or as a substitute for conspecifics – as occurs in Irene Pepperberg's study of the African Grey Parrot[9] or *via* the manipulation of proxy models of conspecifics:

> Such models must be similar enough to the animals in question, and versatile enough in their signalling behaviour, to act as transmitters of information *via* whatever communication system is natural to the animals under study.... Experimental participatory communication might, if suitably developed, provide us with a 'window' through which to learn what the animal is thinking about.[10]

the battleground

The radical divergence in approach between Kennedy and Griffin is representative of the general disagreement in the animal sciences about the possibility and relevance of the investigation of animal minds. The fundamental fissure is between those who see themselves as carrying on a Darwinian commitment to pluralism in their methodologies and those who, motivated by a distaste for Dualism, wish to insist on objectivity at all costs.

One issue, which, more than any other, has been the battleground for this dispute and which illustrates the philosophical nature of the methodological dispute in the animal sciences, is the investigation into whether or not chimpanzees can acquire language. This is revealing. Chimpanzees share all but a tiny part of their genetic inheritance with humans and the battle over this issue shows how close to home we are prepared to erect barriers.

In the 1960s the US Navy made a prolonged effort to teach dolphins to reproduce words appropriately. Despite the fact that the enterprise was abandoned in 1968, a number of similar projects, this time involving apes, began in the 1970s. The object was to discover whether it was possible to teach animals a human language. Various attempts to teach apes to talk had been made long before, but the enterprise took on a new lease of life when, instead of trying to get the animals to mimic human speech, the researchers used Ameslan,

American Sign Language.

The research programmes were prolonged and expensive. They were undertaken with enthusiasm and high expectations on the part both of the researchers and the public. The names of the apes involved became well-known. Washoe took on the star role among the language-using apes, but there were plenty of others: Sarah, Koko, Lucy, Lana and Nim.

Of course we can already communicate with animals by voice and gesture. We influence the behaviour of domestic and farmyard animals by the way we speak and move. At least sometimes, when we encounter wild animals, whatever misunderstandings occur and however deep the mutual incomprehension goes, something happens between us and them by way of alarm and threat, reassurance and submission. The new enterprises were aimed at much more than this. They wanted fully fledged communication, a two-sided conversation in which the animal played, if not an equal part, at least its own part.

Why were such high hopes invested in these projects? The main reason was that if the projects were successful the Dolittlean ambition would be realised. We would be able to talk to the animals. We could acquire the sort of knowledge of them that we enjoy of our fellow human beings.

If an animal could communicate through language all sorts of startling possibilities would open up. The acquisition of language would be bound to have a radical effect on its life. We would have opportunities to alter the life-style of the creature. Just as with human children, the acquisition of language would open up extraordinary potential for growth and development. Once a creature can enter into the linguistic community nothing need prevent it from sharing the knowledge and the values of that community. A linguistic animal could act as interpreter between us and other members of its species. We could send it as linguistic missionary into the wild. The possibilities are endless.

There were other less dramatic but nonetheless valuable prizes to be won if an animal could be taught a language. The ancient, philosophical disagreements about their experience and rationality would be resolved. The outcome of a research programme would determine what had been for centuries the subject of inconclusive debate. If an animal could talk the issue about animal minds would be settled once and for all. No one denies that some animals are more intelligent than others. But many believe that the sort of intelligence manifest in animal behaviour can be explained without appealing to the subjective experience or conscious thought or intentions of the individual animal. Language use, on the other hand, is not compatible with mindlessness. Anything that really talks has a mind. So the general issue of whether an animal has a mind would be answered. What a particular animal actually thinks about, how it feels, what it intends could be resolved, once it can use language, by asking it.

Not only would the issue of animal minds be settled, it would be settled by empirical methods. It seemed that a research programme could be devised, carried out and its findings reported, which would provide an objective route to a final resolution of the debate about the nature of animal minds. There would be no room left for philosophical ambiguity or speculation.

By 1980 the research had run into a quagmire of interpretative problems. The basis of the research was questioned, the methods criticised, the findings challenged. It still has many supporters. But there are intractable critics.[11] Why?

Some critics say that it was badly conducted research carried out by researchers who had a commitment to a particular outcome. These objections are in the same tradition as those surrounding the famous case of Clever Hans.

At the turn of the century there was a great deal of discussion concerning a horse belonging to Herr von Osten in Berlin. Hans was alleged to have been taught to read, spell and do arithmetic, communicating its answers to questions by tapping with a hoof an appropriate number of times or else pointing with its head towards an object or card. An initial inquiry supported the claims. However, Oskar Pfungst, a psychology researcher, eventually established, through a series of sophisticated tests and simulations, that the horse's 'answers' were conditioned responses to tiny and unconscious cueing movements on the part of its questioners. The case became so famous as a triumph of experimental methods in the animal sciences that it was enshrined as a principle. The so-called 'Clever Hans Fallacy' is the fallacy of assuming that complex behaviour can only be explained by the possession of high level cognitive capacities.

According to critics like Terrace, the researchers were guilty of unintentionally cueing the animals they were training and of offering anthropomorphic interpretations of the consequent behaviour. They had not done enough to exclude the possibility that the alleged language use was an illusion. What they were observing was animal behaviour stimulated by the researchers themselves which fell far short of proper language use.

If the issue could be restricted to issues about the standards and validity of the research undertaken, there would be no special problem. All researchers have to satisfy similar criteria. But it became clear that methodological propriety was not all that was at stake. The question was not just whether their methods had been rigorous enough to determine if the animals were engaged in proper language, but what counts as proper language.

Once this question becomes troublesome philosophical issues cannot be avoided. There were different interpretations of what constitutes the essential properties of language. Evidence of abstract thought? talk about absent things? syntactical complexity? linguistic innovation? disinterested reporting? The hope for a final resolution of the animal minds issue on straightforward, empirical grounds was lost in philosophical fog as soon as it became clear that the assessment of the research and its findings hung on intrinsically contestable concepts and theories, including Chomsky's account of language and the propriety of interactive methodologies in general.

So, this most ambitious and hopeful experiment led back to philosophy. One may ask why there was such an investment not only of money but of intellectual expectation in the venture. Does it matter as much as the protagonists on both sides of the debate think? Why should we find it philosophically shocking that animals should speak? Perhaps if we find the very idea shocking we betray a commitment to the idea that language must be a non-natural phenomenon. Whatever is true of chimpanzees or dolphins, mustn't learning to use a language be a perfectly natural phenomenon? After all, though particular languages are learnt, we learn to talk naturally. In chapter 6, we will raise again the question of the relevance of language-use to mind.

conclusion

We have seen in this chapter that three intertwining themes have dominated the history of the animal sciences. How far can the Theory of Natural Selection reach into the lives and experience of particular animals, including ourselves? What, if anything, can we say about the nature of animal minds without lapsing into the dualist conception of mind? What are the appropriate methodologies for the scientific investigation of animals? Under the pressure of these questions, curiosity about the minds of animals, which was such a fundamental motivation for thinkers at the origins of the animal sciences, including Darwin, became eroded. The need to establish investigations into animals as a science meant eschewing the questions surrounding the nature of animal mind and experience. But this has not been the only approach. Especially for those working in Cognitive Ethology, a scientific approach to animals is, and must be, consistent with accepting the reality of animal minds.

Insofar as what we have to say in this book will be of practical interest to those working in the animal sciences, we hope it will help to dissipate the fear that all thinking about the nature of consciousness must be openly or covertly dualist. In this way we hope to provide philosophical foundations for non-behaviouristic methodologies in the animal sciences.

notes

1. A comprehensive and entertaining guide to the early history of the animal sciences can be found in *From Darwin to Behaviourism – Psychology and the Minds of Animals*, Robert Boakes (Cambridge University Press, 1984).

2. *Behaviour: An Introduction to Comparative Psychology*, John B. Watson (Henry Hold, New York, 1967).

3. Quoted in *From Darwin to Behaviourism – Psychology and the Minds of Animals*, Robert Boakes (Cambridge University Press, 1984), p. 170.

4. An illuminating modern discussion and defence of Von Uexküll can be found in *The Parable of the Beast*, John Bleibtreu (Paladin, Forgmore, 1970).

5. *Konrad Lorenz: the Man and his Ideas*, Richard I. Evans (Harcourt Brace, Jovanovich, New York and London, 1975), pp. 160-1.

6. *The New Anthropomorphism*, J.S. Kennedy (Cambridge University Press, 1992). The author was formerly Professor of Animal Behaviour at Imperial College, University of London.

7. *Animal Thinking*, Donald R. Griffin (Harvard University

Press, Cambridge, 1984), pp. 23-4. The author is Professor of Animal Physiology and Behaviour at The Rockefeller University. His most important scientific studies concern migratory birds, the underwater hearing of fish and the investigation of echo-location in bats.

8. *Animal Thinking*, p. vii. Griffin's point is an echo of Darwin's view in that 'It is certain that there may be extraordinary mental activity with an extremely small absolute mass of nervous matter' – *The Descent of Man* (John Murray, 1871; reprinted by The Modern Library, Inc., New York, 1936), p. 436.

9. Pepperberg's research methodologies in avian learning are summarised in 'Social interaction as a condition for learning in avian species: a synthesis of the disciplines of ethology and psychology', in *The Inevitable Bond – Examining Scientist–Animal Interactions*, (eds) Hank Davies and Dianne Balfour (Cambridge University Press, 1992), pp. 240-9. This book is a fascinating anthology of scientists' accounts of their relationships with other animals in the course of their research.

10. *The Question of Animal Awareness*, Donald Griffin (William Kaufman, Los Altos, 1976), pp. 151-2.

11. *Speaking of apes. A critical anthology of two-way communication with man*, T.A. Sebeok and J. Umiker-Sebeok (eds) (Plenum Press, New York, 1980) contains papers from both sides of the controversy.

3: the inscrutable cat

'Of course I can't know what my cat is thinking. I
don't even know what you're thinking.'

introduction

Is the reason it is difficult to understand animal minds the fact that
it is difficult to understand *any* other mind?

When someone says 'Of course, I can't know what my cat is
thinking. I don't even know what you're thinking', she is suggesting
that the problem of other animal minds is just a special case of an
issue much discussed by philosophers – the Problem of Other
Minds.

At its most general, this problem concerns a difficulty in the
notion that any mind (of whatever kind) could know any other mind
(of whatever kind). At this level of maximum generality, the problem is thought to arise not because of any limitation of human
capacities, nor because of difficulties in moving between species,
but because of something about minds as such. Minds are unknowable; they cannot be data for each other; one mind could not be a
phenomenon in the experience of another mind.

Part of the appeal of this thought is that it captures at a philosophical level what strikes us, at least in some moods, as a fact of
human life. Each one of us is finally alone and isolated. We are
intermittently uncertain of other people's thoughts and feelings. We
live with the possibility of deceit, of concealment, of inhibition. The
General would love to know the battle plans of his adversary; the
gambler to know what lies behind the opponent's poker face; the
lover to know how the other feels – *really*. Failures to communicate
may make tragic isolation seem a general condition of human life.

If we reflect on those moments in which our separateness is

borne in upon us, we may conclude that we have run up against barriers that are permanently in place, though we manage to live most of our lives heroically ignoring them. We feel that what we are facing are not transitory or local failures of understanding and sympathy, but permanent and global obstacles to our knowledge of other people. In this way we arrive at the philosophical thought that our relations with others are characterised, quite generally, by surmise, hypothesis, mere belief. Never genuine knowledge.

It is natural to interpret such reflections in a dismal sense. However, a limit is set to this tragic conception of life by the thought that it would be unbearable if it were otherwise. Telepathic powers sound like fun – but they become a nightmare if they can neither be turned off nor resisted. Life for beings as compulsively social as humans depends upon the ability to communicate but also depends upon discretion, reticence and reservation.

In the human case, the Problem of Other Minds is convoluted and paradoxical. In its extreme form – that we can never know anything of others – it is ridiculous; and in its mild form – that there is a limit to what we can know of others – a blessing. It seems both to offer an absurd travesty of human relations and to capture something of life's most bittersweet ironies.

However, on the other side of the species boundary, the Problem of Other Minds appears to be a substantial issue. Scepticism about other *animal* minds presents itself as a straightforward recognition of our actual situation. It demands the attention of the empirical scientist as well as the philosopher and even determines methodologies in the animal sciences. It is one sign of the substantial nature of the animal mind problem that people who give different responses to it adopt different moral views about how we ought to treat animals. Whereas scepticism about the minds of other people is not thought to be a basis for changing our relations with them. Solipsism – the thought that I am the only conscious being in the universe – is the most extreme form of scepticism about other minds; but it can only be expressed in an ironic tone of voice.

Why does the Other Minds Problem strike us more forcefully in the case of other animals than it does in the case of other humans? One explanation might be that in the animal case, the problem does not have a solution, while in the human case it does.

In order to know whether this is true, we need to examine the general Problem of Other Minds. How does it arise? Is it really the case that the problem arises and is soluble in the human case but arises and is insoluble in the case of other animals?

how the Problem of Other Minds arises in the human case

The thought that our knowledge of each other is partial and insecure has been built into the foundations of philosophical systems that have dominated Western culture. It has issued in general accounts of knowledge and belief – in epistemology – and in metaphysical theories about ourselves. Perhaps the most influential account was that offered by the 16th-century French philosopher, René Descartes. According to Descartes, our failure to understand one another is indeed part of a more general condition. There really is a problem about knowledge of other's thoughts and feelings, of other minds. The reason is that we can only claim to *know* those things of which we are certain. This is a familiar and attractive idea. How can one claim to know something and yet at the same time admit that there is an element of uncertainty about it? Unless we have excluded uncertainty, any claim to knowledge is, at best, premature.

According to Descartes, we can see what genuine knowledge is like when we reflect on the knowledge we have of ourselves – of our own thoughts and feelings. In this case, uncertainty *is* excluded. If I am now in pain, I cannot be mistaken about the matter. I know whether I am telling the truth; whether I am the culprit; whether I'm waving or drowning. Compared to this knowledge of ourselves, our claims about others appear remote and speculative. In the case of others, unlike our own case, we simply do not have the right kind of access to the right kind of facts.

As Descartes saw, the flip side of this claim about knowledge is a metaphysical view about the kinds of creatures we are. One of the reasons why Descartes is enjoyable to read is that he appears to be describing, with direct simplicity, our own inner experience – what it is like to be beings like us. Yet lurking within these apparently straightforward descriptions of familiar facts of experience, there are arguments and ideas which are both surprising and controversial. We might develop something like his line of thought in the following arguments.

[A]   Whatever I *really* am is what I appear to be when I
       am *really* known.
       It is only by myself that I am really known.
Therefore: Whatever I really am is what I appear to myself to be.
       To myself, I appear to be a self-conscious being.
Therefore: What I *really* am is a self-conscious being.

[B]   Whatever I *really* am is what I appear to be when I
       am *really* known.
       It is only by myself that I am really known.
Therefore: What I really am does not appear to others.
       I appear to others only as a physical body.
Therefore: What I *really* am is not a physical body.

Both these arguments begin from the same two general principles about knowledge; the first goes on to prove what I really am, on the basis of self-knowledge; the second goes on to prove what I am not, on the basis of the knowledge others have of me. Thus for Descartes it seems to follow from the fact that only I know myself and others do not, that I am a self-conscious being, separate from my physical body; that I am really a *soul*.

It is very tempting to state these arguments in the first person but the conclusion they arrive at is not peculiar to any individual. It is nothing less than the metaphysical view that all persons are mental substances, of a kind quite different from the kinds of things that make up the physical world around them, including their own bodies. This view, that there are two kinds of things in the world, mental objects and physical objects, is called Dualism.

In many ways, Dualism is an attractive account of what we really are. It seems to be true to our own experience of ourselves. Thinking of ourselves as mental objects, uniquely aware of our own states, seems to capture what it is like to be endowed with an inner life and how it is that, despite all the physical changes, we endure as the same person throughout our lives. It has the added advantage, if advantage it is, of providing intellectual foundations for religious aspirations concerning survival after the dissolution of our physical bodies. At the time of the theoretical development of Dualism in the 16th century, this kind of implication was not lost on religious thinkers. However, the innovative thinkers of the age also welcomed the separation of the mysterious mind from the human body.

It rendered the body, human or animal, a possible object of scientific inquiry and technological control. The living body could now be understood in terms of the guiding metaphor of the age – that of mechanism. Dualism was developed not only to save the soul for heaven but to save the body for science.

Dualism seems, then, elegantly to capture our sense of ourselves and of our own identity. It also gives free rein to science in its proper and now undisputed territory. But, as regards our knowledge of other minds, it patently presents us with serious problems. Why?

If Dualism is true, then our knowledge of others is always inferential and mediate. What we know immediately of others is only their observable behaviour, what occurs, as it were, on their physical surface. According to Dualism our claims about others are based on a series of inferential steps, each step a further indication of the distance between us and others. What makes the situation worse is that the beginning and end of this series are in quite different worlds. Somewhere in the process, we have to make a transition from the world of physical things, such as bodies, to the quite different realm of minds and mental states. The mysterious nature of this transition is a prime cause of the difficulties Dualism poses concerning our knowledge of other minds.

These difficulties are aggravated by Dualism's depersonalising of the body. Dualism is ideologically committed to the denial of intrinsic differences between bodies and all other kinds of physical object. But the more we depersonalise the body, the more difficult it is to see how its behaviour could possibly serve as a basis for inferences about mind. If bodies are drained of all significance, and are assimilated to physical objects, what reason have we for nominating them, rather than anything else, as the royal road to mind? So Dualism requires that our knowledge of others depends upon an extended series of inferences. It also makes it problematic for the body to play the key role it clearly must play, if the inference is to succeed.

This, then, is the so called 'Problem of Other Minds'. The position amounts to the general claim that it is impossible to acquire knowledge of any mind other than one's own. We cannot know what others are experiencing. At the limit, we cannot even *know* that they have minds at all.

Of course, practically speaking, we have to behave as if we did have real grounds for believing in the existence of other minds around us and to retain at least a general confidence that we know the kind of thing that may be going on within them. The point of the problem is not that we should give up these natural beliefs. We retain the beliefs that our fellow human beings are conscious, have thoughts, feelings and so on. What the Problem of Other Minds forces us to recognise is that such beliefs are without justification. We must learn to live with the appalling truth that our relations with one another are not founded on knowledge.

the rationalist solution – language

Despite the implications of Dualism for our knowledge of other minds, Descartes himself was relatively untroubled by such worries. He believed that there was an unambiguous and unique sign of the presence of mind – the capacity to be indefinitely flexible in response to the world.

Any natural object behaves in regular and law-like ways and so has determinate characteristics. These fixed characteristics, perhaps the effects which the object has, can become signs of the presence of the object. In the natural world, smoke is a good indication of fire.

In human affairs however, 'no smoke without fire' is nothing but a gossip's charter. Of all the things in the world, the only things that do not manifest themselves in predictable, determinate ways are minds. For Descartes, a creature with a mind is not fixed in rigid patterns of behaviour but is able to act in ways that are quite new and original. It is inherently *rational*. Hence its behaviour cannot be imitated by a machine. This open-ended flexibility is most clearly manifested in the use of language and in the accommodation of behaviour to new conditions and demands. In this way, Descartes gives an unambiguous answer to how we can justify our beliefs about our fellow human beings. Where there is open-ended behavioural flexibility, there is evidence for the presence of mind.

There is something right and important about the thought that there is a deep connection between the nature of mind and capacities to respond to the world in ways which are not specifiable in advance. Versions of this idea are still current, and still controversial, in discussions about what constitutes the distinctive character of human beings. The same line of thought is an essential ingredient in discussions of whether computers could ever think – the Turing Test. Can a machine be so flexible in its responses to questions that its interrogators cannot tell it from a human respondent? In the animal sciences, lack of flexibility is still taken to be evidence that the relevant skills spring from 'mere instinct' rather than genuinely cognitive capacities. Such discussions often pick out, as Descartes did, language-use as the prime realisation of this flexibility – hence, the controversy over the supposed linguistic capacities of chimpanzees.

Descartes set the agenda in thinking about the nature of mind for the next three centuries. Philosophers who were opposed to his solutions nevertheless accepted his way of formulating the problems. Even those who are most aggressively opposed to his conception of the world and of our place in it, can find themselves expressing his ideas in new but disguised forms. However, the success of a scientific approach to the world (which, ironically, Descartes himself helped to bring about) is widely thought to have deprived Dualism of its intellectual respectability. Today it is barely tenable as an account of what human beings really are. Nevertheless, the tenacity of its central ideas and motivations must not be underestimated. Its central ideas have a way of finding expression in views of the world that have officially abandoned it as a relic of a pre-scientific age. In particular, when, in whatever field of inquiry, we are required to reflect on our knowledge of others, dualistic conceptions quietly reassert themselves.

Empiricism and the Problem of Other Minds

This is particularly true of philosophers in the empiricist tradition. Empiricism is founded on the thought that all knowledge derives from and is restricted to sensory experience. (Empiricism will be discussed in more detail in the next chapter.) Since Descartes' soul is not something which can be experienced through the senses, its existence is officially rejected.

However, within Empiricism there are also lines of thought which result in the re-emergence of the Problem of Other Minds. This occurs because the categories of experience and objects which can be experienced are mutually exclusive. Consequently, the experiences of others cannot themselves be objects of experience for me. Hence, since all knowledge is founded on what we can experience, there can be no knowledge of the experience of others. Thus the Problem of Other Minds returns. This time however it is more threatening. Empiricist thinkers are less confident than Descartes about the unique status of language-use and rationality and so are reluctant to use these capacities as a bridge to cross the gulf between self and others. Consequently they look for new means of crossing the divide.

the empiricist solution – the Argument from Analogy

One bridge over the divide which empiricists are prepared to cross is the Argument from Analogy. The upshot of this argument is that our ordinary beliefs about others *are* justified. The justification consists in reasoning by analogy from our own case to that of others. In my own case, I know that my inner experiences are connected to observable states of my body or features of my behaviour. I feel embarrassment and am aware that I am blushing. Later, I see you blush and it now seems reasonable to make the inference that when you blush you feel the way I do when I myself blush. The brick falls on my foot. I feel the pain and I leap up and down. Another time, I see the brick fall on your foot, and see you leap up and down. I then make what seems to be the reasonable inference that your case is analogous to my own. In between the two observable events, there occurred an unobservable mental event – you felt the pain. I know, therefore, that you must be, like me, a creature who can feel pain – another mind.

the Problem of Other Minds in the animal case

We have seen that the effects of Descartes' meditations were in the first place to open up a rift between the human body and the human mind, and then to bridge the rift by appealing to the unique status of rationality and language-use. Empiricism, though officially hostile to Descartes' conception of mind, also finds itself with a problem about our knowledge of each other's minds, but its preferred solution is the Argument from Analogy. In the case of humans, though the problem does arise, it can be solved. We can know that other human beings have minds and we can know, at least in principle, what others are thinking and feeling.

How do these considerations affect our knowledge of other animal minds? If animals do have minds, then the same problem arises and for the same reasons. But can it be solved in the same way?

the failure of the rationalist solution in the animal case

What Descartes actually intended to say about animals is a perennial topic of scholarly debate. Perhaps the safest opinion is that Descartes does not really have a single consistent story to tell about animals. He has two stories which are incompatible. In his more modest moments he is satisfied with agnostic remarks:

> But though I regard it as established that we cannot prove there is any thought in animals, I do not think it is thereby proved that there is not, since the human mind does not reach into their hearts.[1]

However, when he is at his most forthright, he flatly denies that animals have minds. We are supposed to know this because of the absence of that flexibility which is distinctive of mind. In particular, they do not speak. They are natural automata; Nature's clockwork. Notoriously, this has alarming implications for how we should treat animals. Descartes is, with justification, held responsible for some of the appalling cruelty to animals that was inflicted in the physiological and medical research of his own time.

However, Descartes' was made aware of the resistance to both versions of his view of animals. He took this resistance seriously enough to trace its origins to illusions about animals to which he thought common-sense was naturally prone – a strategy, that as we saw in chapter 2, was to be followed by animal scientists in our own times.

Descartes diagnosis hinges on the recognition that humans and animals share a common physiology. When, for example, we are frightened, we are aware both of the occurrence of physiological events, such as trembling, and of the psychological event, the feeling of fear. Descartes thought that because we are aware of both types of event, we take the physiological events to be natural bodily signs of the psychological events. That is, if we see human beings trembling, we are disposed to believe that they are undergoing the distinctive experience of fear. So we come to believe that trembling is a natural bodily sign of the experience of fear. Generalising this pattern, we conclude that particular physiological events are natural signs of psychological events, just as smoke is a natural sign of fire. When we observe these or similar physiological events in animals, we treat these too as the natural signs of psychological events. Thus we are led to attribute psychological states to animals.

Descartes believed that this pattern of thought is a complex of errors and that the error began in the account of our own case. We are wrong to regard physiological events as natural signs of psychological events. There are, in reality, no natural bodily signs of psychological events. As we saw before, genuinely psychological events can manifest themselves only *via* the use of universal tools like language and not *via* determinate and predictable behaviour. If there were natural bodily signs of psychological events then the radical distinction between mind and body would be undermined: the body would be suffused with the mental and inseparable from it. Descartes' Dualism of mind and body would no longer be tenable and physiology could no longer treat the body as a merely physical system.

Descartes felt able to conclude, for these reasons, that our natural beliefs about animals are systematically mistaken. We have no reason to think that non-language-using, non-rational animals have inner mental states – there are no animal minds for us to know or fail to know. The Problem of Other Minds does not arise in their case. Consequently, the rationalist solution to the problem of other animal minds, is inapplicable.

What if we think that Descartes was wrong about animal minds? After all, Descartes himself does sometimes suggest that their existence remains a possibility. Is his solution to the Problem of Other Minds in the human case, still available for our knowledge of animals?

It is not. The cases where animals do seem to exhibit the kind of flexible behaviour required by the rationalist solution remain highly controversial. This is especially true of the use of anything resembling language. In the animal sciences, Morgan's canon (see p. 26), requires that we try systematically to discount evidence for such behaviour. If, nevertheless, we hold that animals do have minds, then we are obliged to hold that they are kinds of mind which do not show themselves through the kinds of signs that the rationalist requires. For this reason, if we believe that animals have minds, the rationalist solution to the problem of knowing that they do and knowing what they are like, is unavailable.

the failure of the Argument from Analogy in the animal case

If we believe that Descartes was wrong about animals, we may, like the Empiricist, turn to the Argument from Analogy. Can analogy be used as a bridge from the human to the animal mind?

It seems that this argument too cannot succeed in the case of non-human animals. The Argument from Analogy depends upon seeing similarities between the way things happen to be in one case and the way that they happen to be in another. If there are observable similarities then the analogy holds and our beliefs about the mental life of others are justified. If there are not similarities, our beliefs, no matter how much we need them, cannot be justified. When we compare ourselves with non-human animals, the basis of the analogy, namely the similarity between our own and the other's physiology and behaviour, becomes unsure. The Argument from Analogy depends upon similarities which, at a sufficient distance from our own case, are simply absent.

We now admit that in the past we have been led into dreadful mistakes about animals because we have mistakenly read superficial correspondences between us and them as underlying similarities. Research in ethology is partly concerned with correcting these errors. For example, what seems like a clear case of parental affection in migratory birds is exposed as something altogether more alien when we observe that if the time for migration comes, they leave their chicks to starve. Again, we admire the alertness of the frog as it flicks the passing fly out of the air with its tongue until we discover that its tongue is directly wired to its retinal movement. What looked like the skill of the hunter turns out to be the efficiency of the trap.

When we recognise such errors, we become suspicious of relying on correspondences between our behaviour and physiology and that of other animals to draw conclusions about the nature of their experiences. The more remote from us an animal is, the less confidence we have in these correspondences. So the force of the Argument from Analogy peters out, quickly or slowly depending on how strict are the standards of evidence we demand. In any case, it can provide no reliable basis for genuine knowledge of animal minds.

The line of thought we have examined insists that there is a genuine Problem of Other Minds; that the Problem is solved by the Argument from Analogy in the human case; but that it survives unsolved in the animal case. The Argument from Analogy is meant to operate as a means of providing a justification for our ordinary beliefs about other human beings. Although it is supposed to function within human territory, it fails to carry us across species boundaries. This is the reason we cannot understand animal minds.

The failure of the Argument from Analogy to reach beyond our species boundaries is the crucial juncture in the attempt to take seriously the diversity of mind. It provides the reason for thinking that the problem of other animal minds is what is left of the general Problem of Other Minds, once it is solved in the human case. It is this position that underlies dominant methodologies in the animal sciences. Science is concerned with knowledge. Since, we cannot *know* that other animals have minds *science should proceed on the assumption that they do not*. If the scientific enterprise can be carried out using this assumption, then the assumption will have been proved correct. It will have been demonstrated that the diversity of mind is an illusion.

why the Argument from Analogy fails in the human case too

This position depends on the existence of the Problem of Other Minds and on the general coherence of the Argument from Analogy. However, as we shall now see, even within the human case, the Argument from Analogy has fatal flaws.

In the first place, if the Argument from Analogy really did what it purports to do, it would involve an outrageous generalisation from my own case. How can I be justified in concluding that because I think and feel, then those around me, who seem to look and behave as I do, also think and feel? Normally, when we move from our own case to that of all others we need some sort of independent evidence that my own case is not unrepresentative, that I am not unique. It is reasonable to conclude from the fact that, if I am made ill by the 'flu virus, that lots of others will be too; it is hardly reasonable to believe that because I have green eyes, everybody else does too. This is because there are backgrounds of knowledge which lead us to expect different results in these cases. But, officially at least, the

Argument from Analogy has no such backdrop of evidence to which to appeal. This is why arguing from the presence of mind in my own case to that of others involves not learning a prudent lesson from my own case but balancing an outrageous generalisation on a pin of evidence.

Secondly, a genuine argument from analogy allows us to form a reasonable belief about an event on the basis of a similarity we detect between it and another event of which we already have knowledge. Off the Scottish coast, when seagulls fly inland, a storm is imminent. The connection has been well established in the past; we reasonably rely on it to be repeated. On the basis of this connection, we can reasonably expect bad weather when, off the Chilean coast, seagulls fly inland. As the occurrence of storms is confirmable independently of the flight of the birds we shall eventually know whether our argument from analogy was as sound as we had hoped. It may be that some feature of Chilean birds or Chilean climes may frustrate our expectations – the argument relies entirely on similarities established experientially. It may be that we never actually confirm the occurrence of the storm. But even if we don't, we could.

In the case of an analogy to other minds this possibility is absent. There is *absolutely* no other reason on offer for believing in the subjective experience of others than the similarity of observable events. There is no other way to confirm the existence of the minds being inferred than the analogical reasoning itself. Hence the argument is very different from ordinary analogical reasoning.

Of course, no one who accepts the Argument from Analogy feels that they are making such an unsupported and extravagant inference. On the contrary, the argument appears economical, modest and realistic. If I want to know how you feel about so-and-so, I can usefully begin by asking how I would feel in your shoes. At least sometimes we are better able to understand others because we have experienced what they are now undergoing. In ordinary life then, we often move from how we feel about things to how others feel in similar circumstances.

But we cannot appeal to the facts of our normal lives to prove that there *are* others in any circumstances at all. This is the final flaw in the argument. The initial plausibility of the Argument from Analogy hides the fact that it makes tacit assumptions about the existence of a social world and then uses these as a basis for demonstrating that we are justified in our claims to know others. But this underestimates what the argument has to achieve. We often need to fill gaps in our knowledge of others; it is a quite different project to prove that there is a gap to be filled. The office-worker may infer from the fact that he finds letters in his pigeon-hole that other people also receive letters in their pigeon-holes. But, should he come to doubt the existence of pigeon-holes other than his, receiving his mail will be no help at all.

The reason for this is that the argument depends on a tacit appeal to knowledge of the existence of others and the quality of their experience. It is this undeclared appeal to our ordinary experience of others which explains how the Argument from Analogy in the human case appears to be plausible.

Consequently, the Argument from Analogy fails in its mission to provide a rational foundation for our ordinary beliefs about other minds. If we accept the question posed by the Other Minds Problem, the Argument from Analogy fails to answer it. It involves a distortion of ordinary analogical reasoning and is circular, depending upon that very knowledge of others which it seeks to justify.

Even on its own terms then, the Argument from Analogy fails to solve the problem. This suggests that we should re-examine the question which the Argument from Analogy tries to solve. Even in the human case, is there a problem about our knowledge of other minds which needs to be solved?

knowledge and certainty

An underlying assumption of the Problem of Other Minds is that knowledge and *certain* knowledge are the same thing. Certainty is regarded as the hallmark of genuine knowledge. But when we look around for knowledge of this kind we find it only in a few places. From ancient times, it has been thought that certainty is a characteristic feature of abstract subjects such as logic, arithmetic or geometry. But, as Descartes stressed, the domain in which certainty is most assured is the immediacy of our awareness of ourselves. Surely, our awareness of our own mental states is the best sort of knowledge on offer?

Here we find a paradigm of knowledge which appears to possess the hallmark of certainty. But now, all other claims to knowledge become suspect because they cannot meet this standard. In particular, our beliefs about others look uncertain because they are based upon a series of inferences. Not only must we establish how the world is on the basis of how the world appears to us to be but we have to make a further move still: on the basis of what we see on the surface of particular parts of the world, namely human bodies, we have to draw conclusions about the conscious activity going on beneath. And so, our beliefs about other minds appear doubly speculative, chancy, presumptuous. In this way, our remoteness from others is a direct consequence of the equation of knowledge with certain knowledge.

When we reflect on this line of thought, it becomes clear that the whole structure is under strain. First of all, our awareness of our own conscious states – which is held up as the ideal of knowledge – lacks many features other than certainty which are also part of the concept of knowledge. Immediate self-awareness is not communicable, storable or checkable by others. It can neither be slowly learned nor suddenly forgotten. If something is to count as knowledge there must be more to it than just certainty.

In fact, once we lose the fixation with certainty, we see that our beliefs about ourselves become more like knowledge the *less* closely they are tied into immediate self-awareness and the more they are connected with the public world. If I am suffering from toothache, it is hard to entertain a doubt about it. Nevertheless having a toothache is a kind of suffering, not a kind of knowledge. On the other hand I can know that I have met Michelle Pfeiffer, even though there are numerous ways in which I might be mistaken.

Knowledge cannot be restricted to those matters about which doubt is inconceivable. If we are claiming to *know* something, our beliefs had better be true. But there is no requirement that it quite impossible for them to be false. Only in specialised contexts is it the case that true things we say could not possibly be false – in arithmetic or geometry. In such fields, for something to be shown to be true *just is* to exclude all other possibilities. Outside of these special domains, if we restrict ourselves to saying what could not be false, we end up saying nothing at all: the kind of certainty that Descartes had in mind has to be excluded if we are to be said to know anything.

In fact, endless trouble is caused by exporting the kinds of justification of belief appropriate to the restricted zones in which certainty is possible to quite different kinds of inquiry. It is even worse if these standards are required of inquiry in general.

Once we have lost the fixation with knowledge as certain knowledge, we no longer feel compelled to compare unfavourably our beliefs about the psychological states of others with our beliefs about our own states. We are no longer tempted by the comparison with an illusory ideal of knowledge. One motive for seeing the Problem of Other Minds as a serious challenge to our relations with others has been removed. Our knowledge of others may be uncertain, insecure, without guarantee, but for all that, and not without all that, it can still be knowledge.

Dualism

A second and more serious weakness in the Problem of Other Minds is the extent to which it assumes the truth of an untenable theory of what our own and other minds actually are. Statements of the problem have to be framed in terms of mind and body, dualistically conceived as independent entities between which there is only a contingent and not a necessary connection.

Why does the Problem of Other Minds require the truth of Dualism? The problem only emerges if we are not able to see psychological states in bodily states. The external behaviour must be regarded as a mere sign of the life within. What we are supposed *really to see* is not the glib smile but the movements of the facial muscles which may or may not be connected with an emotion beneath. If I can *never* see the feeling in your face, then it must be *impossible* for your face to embody what you feel. And this can only be true if body and mind are separate entities. And this is Dualism.

Dualism is widely regarded as an unacceptable account of the nature of mind. Though there are disagreements about the point at which it fails and why. One obvious objection to Dualism is the thought that if mind and body are separate entities, it is impossible to understand how they can interact. And, at least in some sense, they plainly do interact. When I decide to move my arm, my arm moves. When my arm is injured, I feel the pain. Dualism is constitutionally incapable of explaining this basic fact of our existence.

Such criticisms focus on weaknesses in the dualist story. However, the problem of interaction between mind and body is perhaps the least significant and the least interesting of Dualism's weakness as an account of mind. If the failures of Dualism are to prove instructive about our knowledge of other minds, we need to be aware of its deeper, structural inadequacies.

the unworldliness of the dualist mind

The mind, as conceived by Dualism, just happens to find itself in a world of independent orders and objects. Because the mind can exist independently of the body, the fact that the mind is capable of perceiving a world is merely an accidental feature. The perceptual systems of the body, through which the mind is in contact with an independent world, are not integral to it but are, as it were, bolted on as an optional extra. The dualist mind can exist without a world, content with its own internally generated ideas. It is self-contained and complete in itself. It is in this sense that the dualist mind is unworldly.

The unworldliness of the dualist mind is deeply curious. For it denies what most of us would take to be the most important fact about minds – we are not only in the world but we are aware of the world as something distinct from ourselves – there is a world for us. This insistence on the unworldliness of the mind can corrupt our understanding of animal minds. In thinking about the nature of animal minds, we will need to give full weight to the worldliness of mind – the fact that there must be a world *for* the creature.

the unmindliness of the dualist body

If the dualist mind is unworldly, the dualist body is unmindly. The dichotomous choice that Dualism forces upon us, means that the body is drained of all psychological properties, of the inherent significance we normally see in it, of the intentions it manifests, the mental states it embodies. Traditional criticisms of Dualism have concentrated on the weirdness of the dualist mind but the dualist body is an equally alien entity. The body becomes the same kind of thing as any other physical object, differing from tables, mountains and rivers only in degree of complexity. Dualism asks us to think of the body as the shell of the soul.

The dualist split makes it impossible to give a coherent account of whole classes of psychological states. For example, intrinsic to the great run of emotions are typical behaviour patterns, characteristic physiological states and the direct experiences of the person who undergoes them. For the dualist this is metaphysical anarchy:[2] an emotion is either a state of the body or a kind of thought or perhaps a kind of choice. He may interpret fear, for example, as nothing other than a bodily perturbation. But this discounts the extent to which emotional states are ways of experiencing the world. Conversely, fear may be seen as merely thinking of the world in a certain way, as dangerous perhaps – the price of this view is to reduce emotion to a belief; to avoid this choice a third alternative is to think of emotion as a way in which our choices present themselves to us. But this denies the plain fact that emotions *move* us.

Each of these interpretations is partial and fails to accommodate the insights of the others. Once we lose the impoverished dualist body, emotions can be thought of as ways in which embodied creatures and their worlds get a hold on each other. There has to be a way of embracing all aspects of our affective lives. Dualism, with its shell-like body enclosing a clandestine soul, is constitutionally inadequate for the task.

What this failure of Dualism shows us is also important to our understanding of animal minds. The psychological significance of the body does not lie inside it; it is a question of what it does or undergoes. A smile is a smile, it has the significance it has, not because it is the effect of some inner cause, but because of the kind of action or response that it is. This is as true of animal bodics, as it is of our own.

minds, not things

Underlying these failures of Dualism is not the fact that it regards the mind as a mysterious kind of thing which has mysterious kinds of relations with other things. The problem is that it regards the mind *as a kind of thing* at all. It wants to insist on the distinctive nature of the mental. Yet it sees the mind as a thing in itself alongside physical things in the world. It wants the mind to be real, part of the fabric of the world. But its only conception of the real is the kind of reality that physical objects have.

If we insist on treating minds as if they exist in just the same way as physical objects exist, we are in the end forced to produce a bizarre entity – something which is modelled on physical substances and resembles them in every respect except that of actually being physical.

This raises a fundamental question. What is distinctive about physical objects is that there can be different points of view upon them. What is distinctive about minds is that they constitute particular points of view on the world. What we lack – and what Dualism merely glosses over – is the notion of different points of view on points of view themselves. The true nature of physical objects consists in whatever they are, independent of any particular point of view upon them. The objectivity of things demands a distinction between reality and appearance; between how things are and how they appear to be. But how is this distinction to be applied to mind itself? The nature of mind is not whatever it is, independent of any particular point of view. On the contrary, what it really is, is apprehended from some particular point of view. In more familiar but no less mysterious terms, the question is how can we be objective about the subjective?[3]

This difficulty is a profound one; how to form an objective conception of mind. How can we picture the mind from the outside, from any one of a range of possible perspectives, without losing just what appears so distinctive about mind – namely the special status that one particular perspective has?

conclusion

What all this means is that the problems that face us when we think about animal minds are not the traditional philosophical problems concerning knowledge of any other mind. In reality, there is no general philosophical problem concerning other minds. The thought that there is such a problem rests upon a mistaken and unworkable conception of what it is to have a mind and what it is to have a body. We are not mysterious substances hiding within our bodies. We and other animals are living organisms that move and are visible, in the world and to each other. Trying to infer the existence and character of minds from the behaviour and activity of bodies is not only redundant but distorts the nature of our relations with other sentient creatures. One can only feel that there is a problem if one misunderstands, as the Western philosophical tradition has, the concept of mind and if one is desensitised, perhaps as the result of special training, to the distinction between living bodies and lifeless things. This means that dominant methodologies in the animal sciences, which depend upon the existence of the Problem of Other Minds, and the absence of a solution to it in the case of animals, do not have the philosophical justification to which they lay claim.

If one escapes these dangers, the Problem of Other Minds loses its threatening force. But then we can see that the problem does contain important insights, though, as it were, in the wrong key. The thought that our relations with each other are not founded on *certain* knowledge is an important one. But the absence of this foundation need not be lamented. It might instead open us to the liberating thought that our relations with each other are not founded on *knowledge* at all. But if not, what are they founded on? And what are the implications for the attempt to take seriously the diversity of mind? This is a topic to which we shall return.

Still, the problem of animal minds is not the Problem of Other Minds, writ small and furry.

notes

---

1. Descartes: Letter to H. More 1649. René Descartes (1596-1650) is the founder of modern philosophy. He was born at La Haye in France but spent most of his life in Holland before finally settling in Sweden. He made seminal contributions to philosophy, mathematics and geometry and he published work across a whole range of then embryonic sciences. He is most famous for his 'method of doubt', a process of systematically doubting everything that can be doubted, through which he was able to arrive at the conclusion 'Cogito ergo sum' – 'I think, therefore I am'. The certainty of our knowledge of our own existence is the foundation of the theory of mind named after him – Cartesian Dualism.

2. '...The earliest judgements which we made in our childhood, and the common philosophy later, have accustomed us to attribute to the body many things which belong only to the soul, and to attribute to the soul many things that belong only to the body.' Descartes to de Launay, 22 July 1641, *Philosophical Letters*, (ed.) Anthony Kenny, p. 109.

3. *The View From Nowhere*, Thomas Nagel (Oxford University Press, 1986). This book continues Nagel's work on the concepts of objective and subjective viewpoints.

4: the alien octopus

'How could we possibly know what it's like to be an octopus? We have nothing at all in common.'

What on earth can we make of the mind of an octopus? How can we even contemplate acquiring knowledge of the inner life of an animal so different from ourselves? This down-to-earth thought – that we should stick to what is close – is systematically expressed in the powerful tradition of Empiricism. In the animal sciences, Empiricism has supported approaches and methodologies which try to show that the diversity of mind is an illusion. In this chapter we shall have to try to understand this connection. However, as we shall see, Empiricism also contains ideas which may make it easier for us to take the diversity of mind seriously.

knowledge limited to experience

What we can claim to know, says the empiricist, cannot extend beyond what we are capable of experiencing. Knowledge arises from and only from our encounters with our environment through sight, sound, touch and our other senses. Empiricists are in the business of exposing bogus claims to knowledge. Traditionally, their role has been to debunk human pretensions to knowledge of a supernatural order. But equally they have tried to chart the limits of what we can know within the natural order. If God is above and beyond human knowledge, the octopus is *below* and beyond. As we shall see, this tradition of thought has been very influential in the methodology of the animal sciences.

According to Empiricism, what human beings *in fact* know is limited by what we have, to date, experienced; what human beings *can* know is limited by what we can imagine on the basis of experience. We do not, in fact, know about the experience of an

60

octopus because we have not had octopus experiences. *Could* we know anything about the experience of an octopus? Only if we could imagine it. In trying to imagine it, could we draw on anything in our existing experience?

Some philosophers think not: in using our existing experience as a basis for imagining what it would be like to be an octopus, we inevitably succeed only in imagining what it would be like *for us* to be octopuses. While we can endlessly cut and paste our experiences, we can never escape the fact that it is our own experience that we are cutting and pasting. Only if that escape could be effected, could we claim that we can imagine what it is like to be an octopus. Failing to escape means that we can only imagine what it would be like for us to be octopuses. And that is something very different from what it is like for the octopus to be an octopus.

imagination

This reason for believing that we cannot imagine being another creature requires some reflection. Empiricists see no problem in the idea of someone imagining themselves coming to have experiences very different from their ordinary experiences. For example, in the horror film *The Fly*, the actor Jeff Goldblum played a man gradually turning into a giant fly. To do this, the actor and film crew had to prepare for the horrifying climax in which the process is completed. Perhaps Goldblum and the special effects and model technicians studied the eating habits of flies and so on – there are many sophisticated versions of what is, in effect, putting on a fly costume. But there really is something that even the most talented performer cannot do. No amount of method acting or technical ingenuity can enable anyone to imagine *being* a fly. We might try to express the impossibility of achieving this by saying that what we are trying to imagine is what it is like for the fly to be a fly. But this we cannot imagine. Either one is a fly or one is not. If one is, there is no room (or need!) to imagine. If one is not, there is no possibility of success. So, if there is anything it is like to be a fly, and there may not be, it is in principle unimaginable.

This imaginative impossibility is believed by some philosophers to explain why any talk about the experience of non-human animals is inevitably anthropomorphic, why we cannot use our experience as the basis upon which to imagine the experience of another creature.

However, this won't do. The argument proves too much. Using the same reasoning we could show that it is impossible for one human being to imagine anything about the experience of another human being!

Suppose we want to imagine how someone else is feeling, for example, how they took an insensitive remark. According to this reasoning the best I can do is to imagine how I would have taken the remark. I cannot imagine how he would have taken it because I cannot imagine my being him. Not being him, I can only imagine myself being upset or resentful. And so my attempt at empathy inevitably fails.

Most of us are unwilling to accept this application of the argument to the human case. We believe that we can imagine what someone else is feeling. This may be difficult but failure is not inevitable. To imagine another's feelings we do not first have to imagine our being him. Nor are we condemned to imagining only our having those feelings. What we imagine is his having those feelings. If failure were inevitable, Goldblum could not imagine being the human character at the beginning of the film, let alone the dipteran at the end.

The argument began with the idea of the remoteness, the strangeness of another creature's experience. But, on closer examination, it becomes clear that its force derives not from the alien character of another's experience but simply from the fact that it is the experience of another. However, the whole point of saying that it is not possible to imagine being another animal is to contrast an impossibility with a possibility – the impossibility of imagining remote experience is being contrasted with the possibility of imagining familiar experience.

But by trying to harden the impossibility of imagining being another animal, we lose the contrast with what it *is* possible to imagine. For by parity of reasoning, it is just as impossible to imagine someone else having familiar experiences.

So the alleged difficulty of imagining being another animal must consist in something more than the logical difficulty of my imagining myself being anything other than myself. If this logical impossibility were the cause of the trouble, we would be talking not about anthropomorphism but about egomorphism: the mistaken belief that everyone is exactly like me.

Still, the empiricist says that systematic anthropomorphism

arises because people persist in overstepping the boundaries of human knowledge. Such trespass into prohibited areas is both natural to the human mind and difficult to detect. The result is that in the case of our thinking about animals, anthropomorphism is more widespread than we think. This may cause little harm in ordinary life, but it is fatal in philosophy, where we must reflect on the truth of what we say about animals and, of course, in the animal sciences, where we aim to acquire systematic knowledge of animals.

Positivism and science

When Empiricism turns its mind to the nature of science, it emerges as the doctrine of Positivism. Where Empiricism stresses the role of human experience in general, Positivism stresses the role of a particular, specially organised kind of human experience, namely, scientifically processed experience. Its fundamental thesis is that all genuine knowledge is contained within the boundaries of scientific knowledge, in our systematic investigations into phenomena and the laws which govern them.

The rigour and discipline upon which Positivism insists has done much both to embed the scientific temper within our own culture and to extend the range of its competence. It has provided a framework which has appealed to scientists because of the way it clearly distinguishes science both from non-science and from pseudo-science. According to the positivist, the road to knowledge is a straight and narrow one. It involves restricting one's claims to knowledge only to what can be tested. Vagueness and generality are to be eschewed in favour of clearly delineated problems and clearly specified methods of solution. Piecemeal sifting of factual evidence rather than grandiose speculation is the key to progress. This is the only way to build well-established, if always revisable, knowledge of how the world works as opposed to useless monolithic systems of explanation which have characterised philosophy and theology.

As a methodology for science, Positivism may have its merits. But it also has weaknesses. First of all, Positivism inherits any defects that exist in the empiricist theory of knowledge from which it springs. It will be important for us to return to this.

Second, where a theory of knowledge leads, a theory of the world is likely to follow. In this case, the theory of *knowledge* rules out knowledge of states and entities that cannot be explored through empirical experimentation. It says 'Let us not waste our efforts on such matters; there is nothing we can know about them'. But the theory of the *world* that follows says 'There is no sense in calling "real" anything that cannot be known'. The states and entities are themselves ruled out. Hence what cannot be contained within science, drops out of the world. The line of argument here is as follows:

1) Only what can be known through science can be known at all.

2) Only what can be known is 'real'.

Therefore

3) Only what can be known through science is real.

In this way, what begins as a methodology of modesty is gradually transformed into a metaphysics of wholesale denial.

What are the things which Positivism first denies as proper objects of knowledge and then denies to exist altogether? The exclusion for which Positivism is most notorious is the denial that there can be any knowledge of values, moral or aesthetic. But Positivism is also committed to the exclusion of subjective experience as a proper object of knowledge. Psychological states, emotions and sensations are deemed inappropriate objects of scientific investigation.

Positivism is committed to the omnicompetence of science, i.e. that there is nothing knowable which cannot be investigated scientifically. The final test of this view is the susceptibility of the human mind to scientific investigation. It is to be through science that we are to know ourselves. But this knowledge has to be acquired in the same way as knowledge of any other part of the natural world. Consequently, if we want to acquire genuine knowledge of the human or indeed any other mind, we cannot rely on subjective reports of what it is like to be in the states or to undergo the processes in which we are interested. The mind must be viewed objectively. Whatever is not susceptible to such objective understanding we can expect to be marginalised and finally denied. What is true of human minds is true of animal minds, in spades.

Behaviourism

So, Empiricism as a theory of knowledge and Positivism as a philosophy of science are both inimical to the study of animal minds. What happens when they influence the animal sciences themselves? The result has been the domination of the animal sciences by the theory of Behaviourism.

Behaviourism began as an attempt to bring the study of psychology within the scientific fold. In this endeavour, it was crucial that psychology should have and be seen to have sound methods of acquiring its data. In particular, reliance on introspection, of first-person reports into the character of psychological states had to be abandoned. Rather, the study of behaviour was to be the royal road to knowledge of minds.

As a corrective to the view that progress in the psychological sciences could be achieved through introspection, however diligent and sustained, Behaviourism was an important departure. As many saw it, the old 'mentalistic' methods had not proved fruitful. In addition, simply as a methodology, Behaviourism does have its virtues. In a scientific context it is often profitable to build hypotheses on the assumption that the data is complete or at least completable. Behaviourism can be just a way of pretending that all the data is available in order to get on with the business in hand.

It is one thing, however, to draw a red line around the data temporarily, in order to make some progress; it is quite another to turn that red line into a permanent criterion of what will count as data and what will constitute progress.

Behaviourism, in its development in the work of Watson and Skinner, began to make the same shift from methodology to metaphysics that characterises its positivist parent. It became increasingly tempting to treat behaviour as something other than a route to the understanding of psychological states. Instead, psychological states were to be *defined* in terms of behaviour; and this behaviour, moreover, was to be described not in the rich terminology of everyday life but in terms of an artificially attenuated range of concepts. So the descriptions produced would resemble as closely as possible the descriptions not of living things but of moving objects. The scientist's quest for objectivity and commitment to testable and therefore economical theories meant rigorously expelling any notions which could not be cashed out in experimental terms. Experiment here meant procedures modelled on those in the physical sciences. And, it was held, terms which refer directly to the psychological and experiential states of other animals cannot be cashed in this way. On this view, any part of our talk about other animals which has not been scientifically validated is spurious. As we saw in chapter 2, this led animal scientists to systematically eschew the use of concepts to describe their observations which it would otherwise have been perfectly natural to deploy.

Though fiercely criticised, Behaviourism survives as a methodology within the study of human psychology. In addition, the debate about the status of Cognitive Ethology is testament to its continued dominance in the study of other animals.

The alternation between method and theory at the heart of Behaviourism becomes even harder to pin down when the alternation itself is made to hop to and fro across the species barrier. Behaviourism began its career as a strategy for avoiding the supposed bias that can creep into introspective reports of human inner life. When, as in the case of other animals, there are no such reports and hence no possibility of bias, to avoid redundancy it retrains as a theory centred on the denial of the inner lives of animals. Should an unfriendly critic insist that animals do have inner lives, Behaviourism can always fall back on its methodological origins. Now it defends us not from the subjectivism of introspection, but from anthropomorphism, which is seen as a sort of collective subjectivism. What began as a scientific strategy has been transformed into an elaborate edifice. It is founded on a large-scale conception of the nature of science, against which it is extremely difficult to launch a co-ordinated attack. For this reason, the denial that Behaviourism is the only or even a suitable method for expanding our knowledge of animal psychology is perceived by its adherents as an attack on the very idea of scientific inquiry into the nature of animals.

In the animal sciences, it may even be tempting for the behaviourist to accuse her opponents of empty sentimentality issuing in anthropomorphism – the application to the non-human of terms that are only true of the human. Anthropomorphism is a weakness of mind unable to stand up to the rigours imposed by the necessity of adopting reliable methods for acquiring real knowledge about the real world. It arises because people continue to believe in the existence of entities not required by science. This accusation would however be somewhat ironic. The behaviourist must believe that the use of ordinary concepts which are normally taken to refer to the inner lives of conscious subjects are applicable to neither animal nor human. Such concepts are as inappropriate in our case as they are in the case of other animals. If there is a mistake, it cannot be *anthropo*morphism. It might be a kind of *pneuma*morphism – the inappropriate modelling of physical systems on spirits!

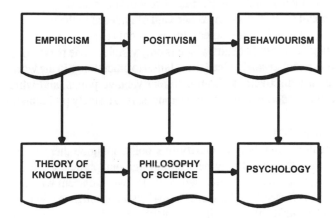

Fig. 4.1 Empiricism and the animal sciences.

One way in which Empiricism influences the animal sciences then is *via* Positivism as a philosophy of science. It emerges in the psychological sciences as Behaviourism which is hostile to the very idea of seeking to acquire knowledge of animal *minds* in any pre-theoretical sense of that term (see Fig. 4.1).

Behaviourism as dualist heresy

One of the curious things that happens on the far side of the species barrier is that Behaviourism and the original dualist theory of mind coincide. Both deny that ascriptions of psychological states to animals are ever justified. Descartes, diametrically opposed to modern behaviouristic theories and methodologies in the human case, nonetheless would agree in refusing to ascribe psychological states to animals. This unexpected coincidence of opinion is not just a consequence of Descartes' belief that God gave souls only to us. In fact, Behaviourism is deeply dualist in its presuppositions.

One of Wittgenstein's (see p. 94) most important contributions was to show how Behaviourism can be seen as a dualist heresy – it portrays itself as a rejection of the tradition but in fact it is a variation on the old themes.

What Behaviourism shares with Dualism is the description that must be given of the nature of mental states. Where they disagree is whether or not anything in fact meets this description. The dualist and the behaviourist agree that mental states, if they exist, must be peculiar mental material. Peculiar because it is a kind of material, like metal or plastic, or any other kind of material in the world, but which, quite unlike any other material, is only ever discoverable by one person. A kind of stuff which is only visible to one person must be very peculiar stuff indeed. Its relation to other things in the world, which are discoverable from different vantage points, and which therefore underlie different appearances, is extremely problematic.

an analogy

An analogy may help to clarify this point. Imagine there were a landscape that could only be seen through one particular window and never through any other window, not even adjacent windows. More puzzling still, to be seen, it *must* be seen through the window. If we go outside, it cannot be seen at all. It is only ever through this particular window and never in any other way that it can be seen.

This is puzzling. If the landscape is really seen *through* the window, it ought to be visible through other windows, and visible without looking through any window – visible directly. But this is not the case. The window and the landscape seen through it are locked together.

What might we conclude? We should think that the 'window' is not a window. The landscape is therefore not something seen *through* it. We might conclude that we are not looking *through* a window but looking *at* a picture. Therefore, the landscape is not something which exists outside what we took to be the window. Once we see that what we took to be a window onto the landscape outside is a picture of a landscape, we are no longer puzzled.

According to the dualist, mental states are accessible only to one person in the same sense that the landscape in our analogy is visible only through one window. Despite this, the dualist is determined to maintain that the landscape is just like any other landscape with the curious but minor qualification that it can only be seen through one window. He believes that there are mental objects which are indeed objects but which are accessible only from one point of view. He thinks that he can take the phrase 'physical object', substitute 'mental' for 'physical' and keep 'object' in its original sense. The dualist may well then claim that the resulting phrase refers to a kind of object, albeit an especially wonderful kind of object.

In the analogy, once we realised that 'window' and 'landscape' are locked together, it was no longer possible to continue to think of the landscape as an object in a world outside. So long as we continued to think of the situation in terms of windows and things seen through them, we remained puzzled; but if we began to think of the situation in terms of pictures, we were no longer confused. We were using the wrong model.

It is commitment to the use of the wrong model that the behaviourist shares with the dualist. They agree that if there are mental states, then they must be real in the way that physical objects are real. Moreover, they agree that mental objects will not be accessible in the way that physical objects are accessible. It is only after they have agreed on these fundamental points that they part company. The behaviourist baulks at the idea of objects that are accessible only from one point of view. Nothing real could be like this. Hence his denial that there are mental states. This is why Behaviourism is a dualist heresy.

The behaviourist, having committed himself to denying psychological states, insists that the concepts that we think pick out psychological states in fact pick out patterns of behaviour. At least those concepts that are not completely infected with mentalistic ideology, must pick out something real. Patterns of behaviour are accessible from more than one point of view and are susceptible to scientific observation and investigation.

But the mistake common to both the dualist and the behaviourist is to model the reality of psychological states on the reality of physical objects. So long as we think of psychological states in terms of physical objects, it will be puzzling how they can be real parts of the world, and yet accessible only in a certain sort of way. Abandoning the attempt to model mental states on physical objects, is the first step in understanding that they are real, and how.

. In our analogy, we ceased to be puzzled when we realised that the landscape was really a picture. What could relieve our puzzlement about the nature of mental states? The dualist has one laudable ambition: to do justice both to the reality of the mind and to its subjectivity. The moral of our analogy is that the price of doing both is to give up the attempt to model the reality of psychological states on physical reality. If we are able to take seriously the diversity of mind, we have to recognise that there are more ways of being real than being real in the way that objects are real. If we are to be realists about mind, we must hold that there is more to reality than that which underlies different appearances.

Empiricism and variety

As a theory of knowledge then, Empiricism restricts what we can claim to know and this results in abandoning the attempt to understand other animal minds *as minds*. But the influence of Empiricism in the animal sciences has not only been to reinforce scepticism about our ability to understand anything of minds other than our own. On the contrary, Empiricism contains ideas which might be thought to make it much easier for us to make sense of other kinds of mind.

Naturalism and continuity

First of all, at the most general level, Empiricism is a *naturalistic* approach to the world. There is nothing other than the natural order which, however complex, is nonetheless a single, unified system of regular phenomena. More particularly, the empiricist is suspicious of any attempt to separate out the human from the rest of Nature. Human beings are neither outside Nature nor some kind of anomaly within.

The empiricist is therefore hostile to theories that try to open up a fissure between ourselves and the rest of the animal world. As the empiricist sees it, these theories stress that some human capacities constitute a difference in kind, rather than in degree: whatever capacity is deemed to be unique to humans – tool-use, language-use, abstract thought – is conceived as indicative of a further, deeper fact about human beings which cannot be explained in naturalistic terms – our rationality.

The empiricist response to this view of reason as a non-natural capacity is first to show that rational capacities are found elsewhere in Nature, albeit in more primitive forms. Thus, they find intelligence, communication, manipulation of objects variously manifested in species other than our own. And second, the empiricist insists that rationality is capable of down-to-earth explanation.

Far from being a god-like insight into the nature of things, rationality is understood as an adaptive mechanism. Like the capacities of all creatures, it is a product of natural selection which, while it has been more or less successful in allowing us to control the natural world, nonetheless is explicable in terms of that world.

So the empiricist does not contrast the rationality of human individuals with the non-rationality of individual brutes. Rather he posits a continuity between the routines of animal existence and the dynamics of human culture. The anti-empiricist maintains that they have nothing at all in common. The empiricist replies that two phenomena can be connected without having anything in common. So long as between them there is a spectrum of intermediary phenomena, we may trace an explanatory connection between them. What *connects* the dawn chorus and the Pastoral Symphony are a million tiny *differences*.

Empiricism and atomism

For this reason, Empiricism involves a commitment to a methodology which invariably produces *atomistic* explanations. This model is inspired and thought to be confirmed by its success in the physical sciences. Whether the empiricist is explaining the nature of the material world, of society, of a language, or, as we shall see, of experience itself, the model will be in terms of discrete primitives out of which more complex realities are to be constructed, according to quasi-mechanical principles. The great advantage of the empiricist construction kit is that it allows for any degree of complexity. The only discontinuities are those between the primitives. And even primitives may prove to be complex upon further examination: what appear to be primitives in one field of investigation may prove to be complex and reducible to other primitives in more fundamental theories.

Of course, when it comes to detail, the empiricist may have to, and may be willing to make compromises. The facts of the natural world may make it difficult to sustain a general atomist programme as a metaphysical principle. But should atomism be overwhelmed as a metaphysical principle, it can be reinterpreted as a methodological principle of economy. Perhaps the phenomenon we are studying is not really composed of fundamental primitives but we shall understand it better if we pretend that it is.

With its easy accommodation of fine gradations, Empiricism is of a piece with the accepted theory of how life evolved on this planet and of the mechanism which drove evolution[1] to produce the diversity we see today. It seems a perfect model for understanding the relations between different species – their phylogenetic ordering. And it need not limit itself to the physical similarities between species. It may also provide the basis for understanding how it is possible for the variety of minds to exhibit gradation.

So, Empiricism has been ambivalent in its attitude to our knowledge of animal minds. It does insist that what we can know must ultimately be rooted in our own experience. But it also claims to possess the theoretical resources to make sense of the experience of creatures different from our own. By breaking down our experience into discrete elements, Empiricism can countenance the idea of those elements differently arranged to form a kind of experience different from our own.

Psychological Empiricism

The empiricist explains the differences between kinds of experience within the animal world in the same way as he explains the physiological and behavioural relationships between different species. Of course he may prefer simply to think of differences in kinds of experience as reducible to differences in physiology and behaviour. This reductionist move turns out to be inimical to the understanding of animal minds as minds.

However, this is not the only direction Empiricism may take. Historically, modern Empiricism began with the philosopher-psychologists of the Enlightenment and early on committed itself to an atomism of *experience*, as well as of the physical world. This aspect of Empiricism leads in a different direction, one that takes seriously the idea of experience different from our own and, in doing so, encourages the development of a theory of mind which is species-neutral, within which a variety of experience is both possible and intelligible.

When, ignoring the human case, the empiricist looks at the kind of variety that characterises sentient life, what does he find? Are there rigid, sharply defined categories? Unrelated clusters of characteristics? Here there seems to be a straightforward answer. All the empirical evidence points to the conclusion that the world of conscious beings exhibits gradation. Outside of the controversial case of human beings, we do not in the natural world find philosophically significant differences of kind between one species and another, between distantly related species or even between classes (*genera*) of species. As the empiricist sees it, outside the human case, species differences are philosophically unproblematic. All the more reason then to suspect that alleged differences between us and all other kinds of sentient life are nothing but special pleading dressed up as metaphysics.

Empiricism offers a more simple and less chauvinist picture. With its atomistic commitments, it seems able to explain the most primitive levels of experience and to proceed from them to the most sophisticated by the familiar route of addition. It therefore appears perfectly fitted to provide an account of the variety of consciousness where that variety is conceived in terms of gradation. Empiricism seems *structurally* adapted to accommodate a crucial difficulty: how it is that humans can occupy a place in the same system of ordering as starfish.

Empiricism even claims that it can explain the variety of consciousness and at the same time make intelligible a distinction that is notoriously difficult to understand and yet natural and compelling: whilst many kinds of animal are conscious, there are a few kinds of animals – notably us and the highest of the higher mammals – whose minds are not merely conscious but *self*-conscious. Just as Empiricism claims to be able to explain how the sentient can emerge by degree from the non-sentient, so it claims to be able to show how consciousness can grow in its scope until it emerges as self-consciousness. Empiricism is so committed to atomistic explanations that it seeks to apply them even to the most unpromising cases of which the 'idea of the self' is one of the most intractable.

It is worth taking some time to say something about this.

consciousness and gradation

Saying anything illuminating about consciousness is notoriously difficult. Articulating the distinction between consciousness and self-consciousness may therefore seem a particularly hopeless endeavour. Many professional and popular works in the animal sciences show a studious reluctance to tackle the issue and instead seek ways to work around it. Their programme can be completed, they hope, without reference to consciousness; other thinkers, philosophers perhaps, who enjoy that kind of thing, may eventually be in a position to throw some light on it. Even studies which set out to communicate to the reader the ways in which animals perceive the world are likely to evade a direct confrontation with questions about the nature of consciousness.[2] Such persistent evasion must make these studies incomplete. As long as we avoid the issue of consciousness something about animal lives will remain uncomprehended. As we are concerned with the question whether we can comprehend animal minds we cannot evade the issue.

Some instructive lines of thought concerning the distinction between consciousness and self-consciousness have been developed by empiricist thinkers (see Fig. 4.2).

It may be thought that self-consciousness is simply a matter of being conscious of oneself. That is, there is something, some kind of entity, behind one's experiences of which, in being self-conscious, one is conscious. On this view, most other animals simply

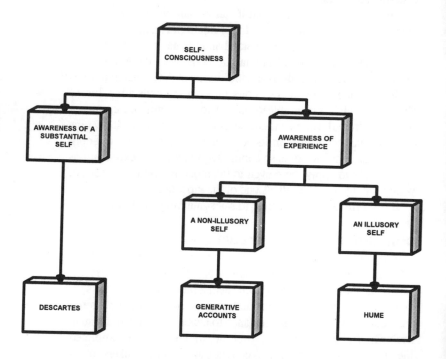

Fig. 4.2 Some accounts of self-consciousness.

do not have such a self. They are not 'selves'. And this is why they cannot be self-conscious.

The denial of self-consciousness in this sense, spreads alarmingly to denials of other more primitive states that we had no intention of excluding. Can animals which are not self-conscious have beliefs or desires? One answer[3] (see Fig. 4.3) is that if Fido believes his bone is in the garden then Fido must be *aware* that he, Fido, believes that his bone is buried in the garden. But, if dogs are not aware of themselves as entities, Fido cannot be aware that he, Fido, believes that his bone is buried in the garden. Hence Fido cannot believe, even at the first order level, that his bone is in the garden. We might suggest that Fido has 'unconscious' beliefs. But, it is countered, the attribution of such unconscious beliefs makes sense only by contrast with the attribution of conscious beliefs. To say that a creature has *only* unconscious beliefs is not to say anything at all. Hence, on this view, it is only through being self-conscious, being able to stand back and reflect upon our beliefs *as our* beliefs, that we can have any beliefs at all. Being aware of ourselves as entities is therefore a prerequisite of having any beliefs.

It has been further argued that, if this argument is sound, we cannot even say that Fido desires the bone buried in the garden or to go for a walk or anything else. How, it is asked, can it make sense to say that a creature desires something if it has no beliefs whatever about what objects or actions would satisfy that desire? Hence animals which are not self-conscious, in the sense that they are aware of themselves as entities, can have neither beliefs nor desires.

Such an account may be thought to suffer from serious flaws. In particular, it may be argued that while animals may not be able to stand back from their beliefs and reflect upon them, it does not follow that they do not have beliefs at all. For even in our case, we must have beliefs, and thus be aware *of* them, before we can be aware *that* we have them and so be able to reflect upon them. That is, if we are to be aware *that* we have beliefs, we must first be aware *of* our beliefs.[4] Consciousness, in the 'simple', unreflective sense, is logically prior to self-consciousness and not vice-versa.

However, perhaps this whole account of 'self-consciousness' is flawed. The most embarrassing defect in the account of self-consciousness as awareness of self is that, as a matter of fact, none of us *are* ever actually aware of something called 'the self'.[5] We are aware of particular experiences but we are not aware of the owner

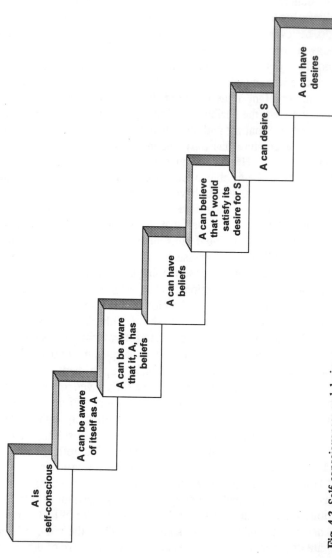

Fig. 4.3 Self-consciousness and desire.

of all these experiences. And on reflection, it should become clear that we *could* not be aware of the self. We can only be aware of the states that this supposed entity actually has. Even if there were a substantial self, separate from all its experiences, self-consciousness could not be consciousness of it. For this reason, there is a need to examine alternative accounts of the nature of self-consciousness.

One view is that being self-conscious is more like being fashion-conscious than being energy-conscious. There would be no such thing as fashion if we were not conscious of it: whereas the electricity bill increases whether or not one thinks about it when one turns on the light. Similarly, the self is something generated by particular kinds of psychological state and does not exist without them. The new sort of awareness does not merely reveal the self to itself. Rather the new sort of awareness in some sense produces the self. Different accounts may be given of the actual mechanism of generation.

For example, it may be thought that from being aware of my experiences as they occur, I come to be aware of my experiences as a set. And when I become aware of the set of experiences, it is natural to think of this set as a kind of entity – the thing which I am. I come to think that I am something more than the sum of my experiences. We should be careful however. If we take this idea to extremes, we start thinking of this sum as something which is completely independent of all its experiences and which could survive all kinds of changes and extravagant transformations. This is how we come to think – mistakenly – of self-consciousness as consisting in awareness of a particular thing, namely the self.

The view that the self is identical with a *set* of experiences presents itself as an account of self-consciousness which is unmysterious in comparison to the rival analysis. Self-consciousness is not a vision of a special kind of entity but just another kind of psychological state.

It is perfectly consistent for this account of self-consciousness to agree with its rival that these reflective states bring great advantages. Only through them can we become aware of our own beliefs and so be able to subject them to examination for truth and consistency. It is only if our beliefs become the focus of this kind of reflection that we can deliberately review and amend them. And it is only if we can do this, that we can be rational. In short, on this view, self-consciousness is a prerequisite for rationality.

It is often thought that this suggestion solves a great many problems. Among other things, it is taken to explain why many animals are not rational. They are simply not self-conscious. Three great distinctions now seem to map on to each other: the human and the brute, the rational and the non-rational, the self-conscious and the conscious. This economy of explanation is thought to be a principal advantage of the claim that self-consciousness is not a special experience of something called the self but is only the awareness of the ordinary experiences we have.

On the contrary view that takes self-consciousness to be the awareness of a separately existing self, such connections are not so easily made. A given creature may or may not be aware of its own self and this self may or may not be rational. It will simply be a matter of unexplained fact. For this reason the analysis of self-consciousness in terms of being aware of one's experience is supposed to be superior to an analysis in terms of consciousness of self.

Incidentally, there is a curious coincidence here. The view we have been examining attempts to put out of business the idea of the self as a separate substance – the religious idea of the soul is just such a thing. Yet the same account has been used by theology to move in quite the opposite direction. As self-consciousness produces the entity of which one is aware, so God's perfect knowledge of Himself accounts for the Persons of the Trinity. Just as our existence as selves consists in our awareness of our states, so in the theory of the Trinity, the very existence of the Persons of the Trinity consists in God's self-knowledge and self-love. Thus the thinkers who support a substantial notion of the self at the human level support a generative notion of self at the divine. Empiricism, ironically, applies this theological notion to terrestrial cases. It is hostile to the notion of an independently existing self which we have and are and which other animals do not have and are not. It is important to understand why the empiricist is so hostile to the notion of a unitary self.

First of all, by definition, the owner of experience will be different in nature from the experential atoms which are its possessions. This will put paid to the atomistic ambition to explain all differences in terms of the combination of discrete but otherwise identical primitives.

Second, and worse, if there is a unitary self that sits behind all our experiences, the empiricist faces an impossible dilemma. As we saw, a defining principle of Empiricism is that all knowledge ultimately derives from experience. Since, by definition, the owner of experience cannot itself be experienced, then, from an empiricist point of view, such a self will be unknowable. But if the self is real but unknowable there will be an absolute limit on the reach of empirical knowledge. The empiricist is unhappy to accept such limits, at least so close to home. On the other hand, suppose that such a self is knowable. This will mean that we can have knowledge of things that we cannot experience and this contradicts the fundamental commitment of the empiricist creed. And so, the empiricist must reject the idea of the unitary self behind experience. His ambition is to dismantle the mind and when all the parts are laid out, they must not include a special component called the self. Experience must be accounted for without reference to the idea of an owner of experience: thought without a thinker.

Hume's bundle

The most notorious, and, for our purposes, instructive attempt to do just this was undertaken by the 18th-century philosopher David Hume.

Hume held that the personal identity of human beings consists in the existence of the relevant connections between successive, but otherwise discrete, mental states. In accord with the atomistic approach, experience is pictured as a stream of independent states none of which occupies any privileged position relative to any other. In particular, there are no special states which consist in acquaintance with some object called a 'self'. There is nothing other than the 'bundle' of experiences.

On this model, 'self-consciousness' is a matter of degree, depending on the number, scope and integration of the psychological states which form the 'bundle' of our experiences. Now, such an account lends itself quite naturally to accounting for gradation amongst minds. The greater the number and variety of mental states a creature has, the more conscious it is. As one climbs along the various branches of the phylogenetic tree, one encounters creatures who do not just have experiences but who have states which have other experiential states, say past states, as their content. We are then inclined to credit them with memory. Along other branches, we come across creatures which are able to take future states as the content of current states and we credit them with intention.

But we also encounter creatures with fewer and fewer states with less and less varied content. The mechanics of selection aside, there is for the empiricist no reason in principle why, at the limit, there should not be a creature with only one experience. There it sits at the bottom of the sea, motionless apart from the slight movement around the mouth parts as the flow of water wafts plankton to its stomach. It has only one sensation. Let's hope it isn't pain.

In reflecting upon his account, Hume admits that he finds it difficult to explain how it is that a series of unrelated experiences are linked so closely together that they generate the illusion of a substantial self. He preferred to profess scepticism about the possibility of a solution to this problem rather than give up the principle of atomistic explanation which had led him to the problem.

Other thinkers of an empiricist outlook may be able to find a way forward. They may, for example, claim that the solution lies in the character of particular kinds of psychological states. What has to be explained is how it comes to be that we take ourselves to be selves separate from the experiences which really constitute us. Perhaps, it may argued, the solution lies in the character of particular kinds of psychological states.

Some psychological states have objects: they are *of* something or *about* something. However, psychological states need not only be about various bits of the world. Some of them, instead of being about trees, antelope or cans of Whiskas, take as their objects other psychological states. Thus we see the tree, but we also may remember *seeing* the tree. We may fear heights or be embarrassed at our fear of heights. This, as we saw earlier, is just what some thinkers take self-consciousness to consist in. In fact, psychological states can form loops each referring to the other. In this way, complex feedback systems of control are developed. These feedback loops emerge in consciousness as peculiar self-referring states. No doubt most are about other mental states. But some of them take themselves as the relevant states. Odd states such as 'Here I am' or 'This is me having this thought' or some such. That is, some mental states take as their content 'This state'. We can come to have such reflexive states at will. And this leads us to misinterpret them: we take them not to be states which refer to themselves but to be states which refer to a particular object, which among its many peculiar characteristics is always present. So, the sense of ourselves as continuing entities distinct from our experiences and our bodies is merely a shadow thrown by self-reflexive control systems.

There can be more or less of these peculiar states. Human beings perhaps have quite a lot of them. The lower mammals rather few. Orangutans and dolphins may have enough so that perhaps they too are subject to the illusion that they are persistent selves, more than the sum of their component psychological and physiological subsystems. Perhaps, just as we are confused about what we really are, dolphins and orangutans are wrong about what they are. In any case there is no doubt that they are self-conscious in the sense that they have psychological states which take other states as their objects.

In this way, the empiricist account of personal identity can be used to explain how the notion of conscious experience can accommodate gradation. Self-consciousness now becomes a matter of degree depending on how many such reflexive states an animal has, how well integrated they are, whether they play an important function in its life, and so on. These states are the atoms of which full-blown self-consciousness is composed. The question 'is this animal self-conscious?' is no more dramatic than the question 'is this man bald?'; it is not an all or nothing matter; it is susceptible to answers ranging from 'very much so' through 'a little' to 'not at all'.

For this reason self-consciousness is no more problematic than any psychological state. And while the empiricist may claim that we do not now have an account of how these states arise, there is a least a way forward. Perhaps it will one day be shown that what appear to us to be sophisticated, unitary states like belief, expectation, or regret are themselves composed of smaller, more 'stupid' components. It is hoped that one day we shall be able to show how these simpler states arise from neurophysiological events and processes. The conviction that such a programme is possible is supported by the fact that the phylogenetic tree appears to exhibit just such a progression; all our explanations have to do is climb back down the tree.

Much the same sort of account can be given of animal thoughts, beliefs and concepts. There are many features of human thought which encourage the view that the capacity to think is an all or nothing matter. Human thoughts can be stored, transferred, transformed, assessed, can form patterns or even complex systems and, above all, be captured in language. These possibilities are intrinsic to what it is for human beings to think. Since animals seem incapable of all or at least most of these sophisticated activities, we feel forced to deny that animals think at all. A conclusion which strikes us as incredible.

The empiricist, however, claims to rescue us from this dilemma. This is because once again he is able to offer an account of thought and belief which admits of gradation. On this account to have a thought is for there to be something going on in an organism, which can count as a *representation* of how things have been, are, or will be in the world. Being frightened of something, expecting something, desiring something, these all depend upon the capacity to form representations of something in the world.

representations

So the simplest elements in the empiricist construction kit of mind are representations: representations are the atoms.

These simple 'pictures' are supposed to be independent of what they represent. Abacuses do not have to be made of wood and sentences describing red pillar boxes need not themselves be red or round. This is because the *content* of representations does not determine their *vehicle*. Consequently, it cannot be essential to any representation that it be in a particular medium.

Nor do representations need to have all the complexity of the things in the world that they represent. A child's drawing of a bus is much less sophisticated than the engineer's blueprint. But both are pictures of a bus. Representations need only have sufficient complexity to enable a creature to do what it needs to do with the object in question; they can be very simple models of a very complex world and yet still function.

On this view, representations are independent of each other. Each stands on its own; it depicts what it pictures. Consequently, representations must bear real resemblances to what they represent. This is necessary because there is no thinker to continually interpret what the representation is a representation of. There is no one to take the representations in one way rather than another. On the contrary, the thinker has to be explained in terms of these free-standing representations and not vice-versa. Hence the only way in which one thing can stand for another is by looking like it, though perhaps in a very abstract, structural way.

Finally, while as a fact of biological life these representations will be essential elements in an animal's capacity to find food, reproduce and so on, being used to do something is not a necessary feature of representations as conceived by the empiricist. They are what they are whether or not they function in the life of a sophisticated creature that puts them to diverse uses. In particular, it is worth noting that representations carry the meaning they have quite independently of any role they may have in communicative exchanges. We shall return to this point in the next chapter.

The reason for the empiricist to support these very abstract claims about the nature of mental representations is that, together, they make it possible for thought about the world to exhibit gradation; an animal can have lots of representations of the world or very few.

Moreover, just as we saw with the atomistic analysis of self-consciousness, contemporary empiricists hope that by making the units of composition small enough and stupid enough, they can show that the representations – the thoughts – can be understood as neural processes which can be described without using psychological concepts. In this way, they can explain how thought goes on without having recourse to the notion of the thinker.

We now see the ramifications of the empiricist rejection of the idea of a separately existing self. Given that there is no 'thinker', to take representations in one way rather than another, it is necessary that the representations themselves really resemble, albeit abstractly, the things they represent. The stability of this resemblance, the fact that something in the world is represented and can continue to be represented, is only possible if the representations are embedded in physical structures.

In this way then, the rejection of the idea of the unitary self comes to be seen as a prerequisite of a *physical* explanation of how creatures come to have thoughts at all.

The empiricist may pursue this ambition of giving a physical account of experience. But, even if he fails, he will still have produced an account of experience which is consistent with the variety that the natural world exhibits. At least at the most general level, the gradation in types of experience can be understood in terms of the number, form and integration of representations. The crustacean, we may suppose, has only a few representations which picture its environment in the crudest ways. We don't imagine that the lobster fantasises or theorises. So what representations it has are directly geared into functions in its life. The representations the lobster has, however they are embodied in its physiology, can be identified, or individuated *via* these functions. In other parts of the phylogenetic tree, the role that representations play is more flexible because it is less locked into rigid patterns of behaviour. So it may prove more difficult to individuate the representations of more complex creatures. Nonetheless the empiricist believes that he has overcome the dichotomous choice between thinking and non-thinking creatures which seemed forced upon us. There is no absolute division between simple neurological representations and conscious experience or between consciousness and self-consciousness. It is all a matter of increasing complexity.

chimpanzees and consciousness

Carrying out this project in detail is very difficult. The difficulty arises because of the extreme economy that the empiricist imposes on himself. The apparently rich and diverse psychological phenomena of the whole natural world, including consciousness and self-consciousness, are to be explained in terms of representations and the causal mechanisms that are supposed to put them to work.

The regime is so exacting that even animal scientists, who regard their research as thoroughly and robustly empirical, embroil themselves in philosophical disputes which, officially, they should have left behind, and end in embracing positions which they officially deny. A striking example is the attempt to determine whether or not chimpanzees are 'self-conscious'.

A common methodological rationale for investigating this question is carried out by seeking to determine how chimpanzees react to images of themselves in mirrors. Chimpanzees are exposed to full-length mirrors for long periods of time. Initially, they respond to their images as if they were other chimpanzees. But after two or three days, their behaviour becomes 'self-directed': they are able to groom themselves whilst looking at their image in the mirror. After a few days, their interest in the mirror-images wanes. Later, under anaesthetic, red marks are painted on the faces of the 'mirror-educated' chimpanzees. On recovery, their interest in their own image noticeably increases and they repeatedly touch the marks whilst looking into the mirror. Chimps who had no previous experience of mirrors, reacted to their own images as if they were seeing other chimpanzees. Similar experiments with orangutans produced the same results. But experiments with gorillas and monkeys did not.

Parallel results have been found in experiments using live and taped television pictures.

Both sets of experiments have been variously interpreted. The researchers concluded that chimpanzees and orangutans but neither gorillas nor monkeys have 'a sense of self'.[6] Other commentators reject this interpretation, believing that the phenomena can be explained without reference to self-consciousness, perhaps by some process of complex association. Their rejection is a variant on the Clever Hans fallacy that we noted earlier. Whatever the merits of this argument, some researchers, for example Jaynes, feel the need to support it with quite different sorts of consideration:

> ...that a mirror-educated chimpanzee immediately rubs off a spot on his forehead when he sees it in a mirror is not...clear evidence for self-awareness, at least in its usual sense.... Our conscious selves are not our bodies...we do not see our conscious selves in mirrors. Gallup's chimpanzee has learnt a point to point relation between a mirror image and his body, wonderful as that is.[7]

The clearly philosophical claim, that we do not see our conscious selves in mirrors, echoes a similar point made by the original researcher:

> ...an organism is self-aware to the extent that it can be shown to be capable of becoming the object of its own attention.... When a monkey grooms its own arm, the monkey is not the subject of its own attention; its arm is.[8]

Reviewing these experiments, Kennedy comments:

> ...[the] self-awareness hypothesis has not been disproved. It is hard to see how it could be proved or disproved. But...[Gallup's] hypothesis has been accepted without ruling out a more plausible alternative [associationist] hypothesis and this indicates an anthropomorphic bias....[9]

These commentaries reveal how tempting it is for the current empiricist view in the animal sciences to fall back into an essentially dualist theory of mind. To claim that when we look in the mirror we do not see our conscious selves but, presumably, only our physical selves, is Dualism running wild. The reason is, that for dualists, the conscious self is never visible, either indirectly in mirrors, or directly. It is visible only to the inner eye.

Similarly, Kennedy thinks, on the one hand, that there is a conceptual impossibility about proving that chimpanzees are self-conscious and, on the other, that it is all a matter of hypotheses which have or have not been proven. His complaint is that something which he believes could never be proved, has not been proved. He is stuck in the traditional Other Minds Problem. For all its empiricist trappings, it is really a thorough-going dualist picture of mind.

If applied to humans this test would mean that even the most sophisticated piece of self-conscious thought, feeling or behaviour would not count as self-conscious. If Jenny is having deeply self-conscious thoughts about what her best friend thought about what Jenny said to her yesterday, it could be argued that this is not evidence that Jenny is self-aware since she is thinking not about herself but only about the thoughts that her best friend is having about her.

In fact, this argument is an application of the general argument against the notion of self-consciousness developed by Hume (see p. 79): none of us *are* ever actually aware of something called 'the self' because consciousness is always consciousness of some particular thing, be it a thought or a feeling – or a monkey's arm. The argument has the effect, as it was designed to, of making the notion of self-consciousness, in the sense of being aware of something called 'the self', appear self-contradictory. Once again, the only thing that might pass this test would be a thoroughly dualist intuition of self, the very kind of experience, which according to Hume, we never have and which the argument shows that we could never have.

In all these cases, there is on the surface an officially empiricist viewpoint that denies any hocus-pocus about souls, and maintains its faith in causally explicable mechanisms of association, even at the cost of scepticism about the ascription of any psychological states to animals. But, as soon as the position is probed, it is revealed as dyed-in-the-wool Dualism.

conclusion

The claim that we cannot understand the experience of creatures

other than ourselves because we have nothing in common with them
has its roots in the philosophical tradition of Empiricism. It expresses scepticism about animal minds because of the empiricist's
insistence that our knowledge is restricted to our own experience.
These views have influenced the philosophy of science and produced methodologies in the animal sciences which are inimical to
taking animal minds seriously.

However, the attitude of this tradition is more complex than at
first appears. If Empiricism can overcome its own sceptical problems and bridge the gap between ourselves and other animals, it has
a theory of mind which is generous enough to house all species from
the most primitive to the most advanced. It enables us to think of
animal minds as both different from our own and yet intelligible
because they are constructed out of the same fundamental elements
which are accessible to us within our own experience. In this way,
Empiricism holds out the prospect of a theory of mind which is
species-neutral.

However, the animal friendly strand will only work if Empiricism is really intelligible as a theory of mind. About this, 20th-
century Philosophy has raised serious doubts. Doubts that we shall
return to examine in chapter 7.

In the meantime, we shall continue to trace the presuppositions
and implications of the ordinary things that we say about our
knowledge of animal minds.

notes

1. See Alec Panchen's study *Evolution* (Bristol Classical Press,
1993) in this series.

2. For example, *Supersense: Perception in the Animal World*
by John Downer (BBC Books, London, 1988) – a companion to a
popular BBC television series.

3. C.f. *Interests and Rights: The Case Against Animals*, R.G.
Frey (The Clarendon Press, Oxford, 1980). The author is known for
his scepticism about the notion of animal rights.

4. C.f. 'Frey on why animals cannot have simple desires', Tom
Regan in *Mind* (1982) vol. XCI, pp. 277-80. The author is a prolific
advocate of the rights of animals.

5. The classic account is David Hume's *A Treatise of Human*

Nature, Book I, Section VI 'Of Personal Identity'. David Hume is the most important classical empiricist and his Treatise was published in 1739, when he was 28 years old.

6. 'Self-recognition in primates. A comparative approach to the bi-directional properties of consciousness' by G.G. Gallup Jnr in *American Psychologist* 32 (1977), pp. 329-38.

7. 'In a manner of speaking' by J. Jaynes in *Behavioural and Brain Sciences* 1, pp. 578-9. Quoted in Kennedy (1992), p. 108.

8. Quoted in *The New Anthropomorphism* by J.S. Kennedy (Cambridge University Press, 1992), p. 109.

9. *The New Anthropomorphism*, p. 113.

5: the 'happy' chimpanzee

'It's all very well saying that you can just see that the chimpanzee is happy. But "happiness" is a human idea. You shouldn't impose human ideas on other animals.'
These remarks express the idea that we don't know much about animal minds. And the reason given is that whatever we say will be anthropomorphic.

Anthropomorphism is not the name of a theory or a doctrine. It simply means representing something in human shape. In the context of thinking about other animals, it is understood as the name of a kind of mistake. It means *inappropriately* thinking of what is not human in terms that apply to humans. We can make this sort of mistake in relation to anything which is not human, not just non-human animals. Like other kinds of mistake, anthropomorphism is sometimes damaging and sometimes quite harmless.

Consider how we describe the inanimate natural world. We call seas 'vengeful', peaks 'indomitable', and redwoods 'noble'. There may have been times when these metaphors expressed primitive animistic views of Nature. But now we use these terms in virtue of an aesthetic analogy between features of these inanimate objects and human characteristics. Such descriptions are harmless and they no longer threaten to distort our view of the natural world.

Basil and his car
The situation is quite different when we describe the inanimate, non-natural world. When Basil Fawlty thrashed his car for failing to start, he was punishing it for maliciously frustrating his wishes. When he gave the vehicle 'one last chance', he was treating it as if it were being unco-operative in a way that only human beings can be unco-operative.

Basil's reaction to machinery is extreme but there is a good reason for it. We attribute what look like exclusively human characteristics to machines because machines really contribute to human tasks. When they 'let us down', our efforts are frustrated because of them. And that frustration is not merely external or accidental. A landslide may prevent us from completing a journey. But as the rocks and the mud did not enter into the travel arrangements in the first place, we are not inclined to think of them as anything other than a problem to be overcome. The car on the other hand was designed precisely to take us on journeys; it always was part of our calculations; without it the journey may well not have presented itself as a possible undertaking at all. Because machines are inherently functional in a way the natural, inanimate world is not, they are absorbed into the human domain. Machinery plays a part in carrying out human intentions. So unlike the case of the natural, inanimate world, talking about machines as if they were privy to those intentions involves more than just a metaphor. Still, we have no trouble generally distinguishing correct statements about *functions* from the anthropomorphic attribution of psychological states or capacities.

One important exception is the digital computer where there seems to be a much stronger temptation to ignore this distinction. It is curious how in some academic circles there is a willingness, bordering on compulsion, to attribute psychological states to machines which is in direct proportion to the readiness, bordering on zeal, to deny such states to animals. It is clearly something requiring a philosophical diagnosis that it comes more naturally to many people to believe that computers could think than that dogs do think. Part of the intellectual temptation here depends upon the willingness to treat the mechanisms of natural selection as if they were the specifications of an animal, in the way that a specification of a machine constitutes it as a computer.

Still, computers aside, we are not fooled when we say that the television goes on the blink just so that we cannot see our favourite comedy show. For the most part we take our humanising of machines neither seriously nor literally.

It is in relation to other animals that anthropomorphism begins to cause real trouble, but not all the time, nor even most of the time. We often use precisely the same terms to talk about animals as we use to talk about ourselves. And we think that we are right to do so.

In fact, the issue of anthropomorphism does not even arise in much of our talk about animals.

We have legs. So do lions, blackbirds and lizards. This is not an example of the anthropomorphic mistake. In attributing 'legs' to them we are not inappropriately describing them in human terms. And it is not even true that their legs are 'legs' because of a similarity to our own. The concept 'legged' applies equally to ourselves and some other animals; it does not belong properly to the human species and only by courtesy to other species. Because this term does not apply only to us, there is no possibility of making the anthropomorphic error. There is room for squabbling about the tentacles of the octopus or the 'foot' of a slug. But the disagreement would be about whether the concept of leg which applies to ourselves and a host of other creatures also applies to these creatures. Certainly, the term 'leg' is a word occurring in a human language. It is a human concept. But this does not mean, of course, that its application is restricted to human beings. Nor does the fact of it being a human concept, mean that it must be applicable to other creatures in some extended or attenuated sense. We neither add to, nor subtract from the sense of the general concept when we apply it to non-human animals.

However, even in this simple case, problematic ways of talking can easily become intertwined with our otherwise unproblematic descriptions. The elegant gait of the gazelle is elegant relative to human notions of what constitutes elegance. But again, this is not a case of anthropomorphism. Though, as an aesthetic concept, elegance emerges in the context of human responses and interests, it does not apply only to the human. Very few humans move as elegantly as gazelles. So speaking of the elegant gait of the gazelle cannot be anthropomorphic because, as we saw, anthropomorphism means inappropriately thinking of what is not human in terms that apply only to humans. We need to distinguish between those terms we apply to animals, the sense of which is constituted by human responses and those terms we mistakenly apply to animals which in fact apply only to humans.

It is easy to think that anthropomorphism is more pervasive than it actually is if we use it as a catch-all for everything problematic in our talk about animals. To avoid becoming unnecessarily pessimistic about our knowledge of animals we must distinguish anthropomorphism from more general problems that are not intrinsically connected with crossing the species barrier.

An example may help to clarify the possibilities. If you are given the following information about Turing (see Fig. 5.1), can you tell whether Turing is a mathematician or a mathematician's dog?

We can reason as follows:

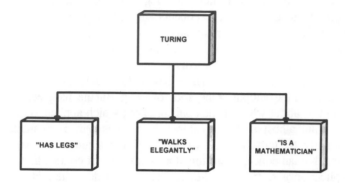

Fig. 5.1 Turing.

a) If we know Turing has legs, it is an open question. There are some terms whose meanings are independent of human tastes and preferences, and which apply equally to human and some non-human animals – they 'have legs' in just the same sense that humans 'have legs'.

b) If we know that Turing walks elegantly, it remains an open question. Despite the fact that what 'elegance' means depends upon human interests and preferences, it applies equally to human and some non-human animals. Many things other than human beings can be elegant. Non-human animals can have an elegant gait in just the same sense as an athlete or dancer.

c) If we know that Turing does mathematics then (leaving Martians and computers aside), we know that he or she is human. There are terms whose meaning may or may not depend upon human tastes and preferences, but which, irrespective of this, certainly apply only to humans and not to non-human animals. It is a moot point whether the laws of mathematics are independent of human interests and preferences, but in any case, as far as we know, only human beings are capable of being mathematicians.

It is only beliefs about animals that involve terms of type (c) that are anthropomorphic. Once we have isolated those beliefs that are genuinely anthropomorphic, it is still necessary to distinguish more or less significant instances of the generic mistake.

In particular, we need to distinguish between naive anthropomorphism and systematic anthropomorphism. The former may well express deeply rooted, spontaneous attitudes towards the natural world but it is innocent of theoretical reflection. The latter is the product of reflection on ourselves and our relation to animals. It is anything but naive – incorporating theories about human minds and human language, the nature of scientific inquiry, and all the ways in which we think about ourselves and the natural world. In the case of naive anthropomorphism there is a further distinction between harmless and harmful cases.

naive anthropomorphism

Clearly, some kinds of anthropomorphism are naive. More than one artistic genre exploits the guileless promiscuity of the imagination. Children's literature is full of rabbits that wear waistcoats and pigs that build houses. A standard device of allegorical paintings, such as Titian's *Allegory of Prudence*, is to exploit connections between animal stereotypes and human virtues and vices. One would have to be in a very puritanical frame of mind to object, in principle, to such genres.

Still even here, in these apparently harmless cases, there may be times when we feel the need to correct the conventional fictions. We can enjoy *Jaws* or *The Jungle Book* but we should remind ourselves that sharks are not really psychopathic murderers and that wolves do not go around in marauding gangs. It may even be that anthropomorphic traditions of story-telling have a more subtle and pernicious effect. They may contribute, as some people believe, to our culture's general attitudes towards animals, attitudes which are systematically corrupted. Perhaps these traditional stories, innocent as they appear, are one way in which we make acceptable to ourselves the global exploitation of our fellow creatures.

This is a controversial viewpoint. There is no controversy, however, about the harmfulness of some kinds of naive anthropomorphism. Domestic animals are sometimes cruelly treated because their owners naively credit them with human vices. The dog's exuberance is misread as malicious rebelliousness which justifies punishment. Perhaps kicking the cat for catching birds involves a milder form of the illusion that led to the mass executions of cats for consorting with the devil.

In these naive forms, anthropomorphism ranges from flights of fancy to illegal cruelty. At the harmful end of the spectrum, anthropomorphism has to be combated in the ways that we attempt to change other humans' errors, misunderstandings or vices – by education and reform. But whether or not we succeed in resisting harmful naive anthropomorphism, doing so does not enmesh us in any distinctively philosophical problems. However, for other kinds of anthropomorphism, different from the naive types we have discussed so far, such straightforward remedies may not be available.

systematic anthropomorphism

Some philosophers – for example, Leahy[1] – claim that anthropomorphism is far more widespread than we think. They believe it is so widespread because our talk about animal minds is corrupted by *systematic* errors. It is not only the sentimental who chat with their budgerigars who are mistaken. All of us are guilty of the same type of error whenever we make what we take to be ordinary remarks about the experience of animals.

On this view, systematic anthropomorphism is not just the naive variety run rampant. It is a new strain produced by prior commitments to false views and theories which are expressly philosophical. These false views are most commonly thought to concern language.

Wittgenstein

The diagnosis of anthropomorphism in terms of misunderstandings about the nature of language begins with the simple observation that it is human concepts we must use when we talk about the non-human. Because this compromises what we say about animals, it gives us a reason to be sceptical about claims to know anything about animal minds.

This line of thought is reinforced by certain readings of the work of the 20th-century philosopher, Ludwig Wittgenstein. Wittgenstein was and continues to be a controversial figure in contemporary philosophy. There is disagreement not only about the truth of what he said, but also about what he meant by what he said. The situation is made worse by the fact that his thinking underwent a radical change so that it is necessary to distinguish his early from his later philosophy. The competing interpretations of his work illuminate different aspects of the problem about animals. In what follows, we explore these different interpretations of Wittgenstein's thought and explain their implications for our thinking about animals.

The distinctive feature of his later philosophy is the view that language can only be understood as a set of interactions within a community of social beings; he maintained that communication is the heart of language. It may seem odd that anyone should have to point out – as if it were news – that language is all about communication. What could be more obvious? What else could language be for? However, we may begin to worry about this common sense view when we are struck by the equally commonplace idea that in order to be able to communicate *with* others, we must first have something *to* communicate to others. How we can say anything to others unless we first have something to say?

Wittgenstein – language as representation

This was the line of thought on which the young Wittgenstein focused. His central concern was not the uses to which we put language, but what looks like the more fundamental issue – what language really is.[2] He argued in his early work that what is essential to language is whatever it is about language that enables us to have something to say. Given that we have something to say, we might then go on to communicate it to others or we might not. We can use language to communicate only if language is up and running; only if we have something to say.

How then does language enable us to have something to say? Having something to say means having something to say about how things are. Language can recreate – represent – how things are in the world. Genuine language is a medium in which we can picture the facts and events of the world. We can say not only how things are, but also how things aren't, and so how things might be. It is because language can represent what could be, but isn't the case, that we can use it to change the world and to gain control over it. We are able to store these representations in permanent forms and so we are able to accumulate knowledge and communicate it to future generations.

The more we reflect upon this, the more representation seems to be the heart of language. And now it will appear that even if communication happens to be the primary purpose to which social beings like ourselves put language, it is not at all obvious that communication is the essence of language. Perhaps there could be solitary creatures who have beliefs about the world which they can express to themselves but which they never communicate to others. On this view then, communication is just one of the things a language-user might do with representations.

So communication is a trade in representations. A trade in public pictures of our thoughts. But what of thoughts themselves? The young Wittgenstein believed that thoughts too are representations, our own pictures of how things are; our own private representations.

Along these lines, Wittgenstein gave a peculiarly forceful and rigorous expression to a view of language shared by many past and contemporary philosophers. In order to have anything to communicate, in order to have any thoughts at all, representation must come first and foremost. And so, not communication, but *representation* is the foundation of language.

The use of the concept of representation to explain the nature of language and meaning has been enormously influential. It has become a fundamental tenet of those disciplines that centre on the cognitive sciences. In the previous chapter, we saw how it was the vital component in the empiricist attempt to make sense of the idea of gradation in types of consciousness: self-consciousness is nothing other than self-representation. But it is also what makes it plausible that eventually we shall be able to give a physical explanation of how consciousness arises. Physical systems like brains and computers are capable of storing representations. Both are representational engines. For this reason it is widely thought that both are capable, suitably configured, of possessing states that it makes sense to call 'conscious'.

Wittgenstein – language as communication

Against this background, Wittgenstein's later claim that there is no language outside of communicative exchanges, far from being a truism, is a seditious idea; it turns on its head the traditional view. The foundation of language is communication. Representing, like warning, praying and joking, is just one of the things we do in our language. The content of what we can communicate to others is not something independent of the possibility of communication itself.

The idea that communication is prior to representation has

radical implications: a language which could represent but which was not capable of use in communicative interactions, a 'private language', is not possible. However rich and various the animal kingdom, it could not possibly contain a solitary language-user who could not share its thoughts with others. And this means that it is no longer possible to take thought itself as a private system of representations. The social character of language cannot be restricted to the public realm. What looks like a straight distinction between the inner essence of language and its public purposes collapses. According to Wittgenstein's later philosophy, what is inherently social is not only what comes out of our mouths but what is in our minds.

Of course we may still keep our thoughts to ourselves, lie, or dissemble. Each of us is more or less closed or opaque to others. We may withdraw or be driven into ourselves, refusing or despairing of communication with others. Nevertheless, according to Wittgenstein, even our most private thoughts are structured by the concepts we share with others. We can hide within ourselves but we cannot vanish from view.

Wittgenstein's views about the social nature of language allow people to be enigmatic, mysterious and isolated. What he denies is not the inner life but that account of the inner life which makes it in principle unsharable with others. He requires us to change our philosophical views about psychological concepts – our theory of mind. As we shall see, the realignment of our psychological concepts along a social rather than a private axis leads to optimistic conclusions for what we can say about animal minds. However, these same thoughts have led others to sceptical conclusions, and to these we must now turn.

our concepts are *our* concepts

The sceptical interpretation begins from the thought that because language is rooted in our social interactions, the meanings of the words we use are fixed by the contexts in which we use them. And these are, of course, human contexts. This is taken to mean that we are likely to get into trouble when we use concepts in contexts other than those which are their normal home. For example, we can tell whether it is half past three or four o'clock in New York or Sydney. But, to use Wittgenstein's example,[3] what are we to say if someone asks what time it is on the sun? Our normal time-keeping conventions cannot be followed in this case.

On this sceptical view, it is this general truth which creates the problem about knowledge of other animal minds. Because the meanings of all concepts are fixed by their contexts, to move outside human contexts altogether is to send language on holiday.[4] This, of course, includes psychological concepts. Our talk about other animal minds is compromised because it is talk about experience in animal and not in human contexts.

Following this train of thought leads to a general problem about applying psychological concepts outside human contexts. But the problem does not arise because they are psychological concepts. It is a consequence of the general truth that when we apply any concept outside of human communicative contexts, we necessarily lose confidence in whether we really know what we mean. There are limits to what we can meaningfully say. To ignore these limits is to embrace a picture of language in which human interests and purposes play no part. Language is regarded as a disinterested representation of reality. But if we admit that human conventions fix meanings, it is no longer plausible to think of language as a cold, clear mirror of reality.

Forsaking this ultra-objective interpretation of language means admitting that our use of psychological concepts is intrinsically context-dependent. When we attribute thoughts and feelings to ourselves and our fellow humans, we know what we mean and we can, generally speaking, determine whether what we say is true or false. But we can do so in virtue of the human conventions that govern the particular ways in which we use those words. Psychological concepts are fixed in exchanges between people. When we learn how to use the concept of belief, for example, we submit to the conventions, the checks and the tests which determine the sense of what we say. As a result, there is nothing vague or undecidable about whether Bill Clinton believes that Al Gore is in the Capitol.

But there *is* something problematic about saying that the dog thinks that the cat is up the tree. It is not just that there is no way of deciding beyond any doubt whether the dog does or doesn't believe this. It is rather that we cannot be sure what we mean by saying he does or doesn't believe it. What is at stake is the appropriateness of applying the concept of belief to the dog at all.

The meanings of our psychological concepts are embedded in our ordinary language. Terms such as 'anger', 'hope', 'pain', 'doubt' and 'joy' have their natural homes in our ordinary ways of talking. Wittgenstein thinks of these complex and overlapping patterns of speech and activity as 'language games'. These social activities guarantee the shared meanings of the words we use but at the same time they set a limit to the domain in which they may be legitimately deployed. It is precisely because the activities are social that the meanings are shared; but equally, it is because we alone (and not members of other species) share these meanings that non-humans are excluded from the domain within which they can legitimately be deployed.

On this interpretation of his thought, Wittgenstein buys human communication at the price of inter-species silence. Beyond our agreement *in* one another through the speaking of language, we cannot be confident that even our questions about non-human sentience have a sense. Displaced from their natural homes in our forms of life, our psychological concepts cannot find gainful employment. To attempt to raise and answer questions about, for example, whether or not the lion is really 'angry' when he springs, is simply to send language on safari.

The proponents of this line of thought are certainly hostile to claims to know about the minds of animals. But they do not think that such claims are false. Rather no claims could be true or false. The focus of the argument is not on the truth or falsity, the certainty or uncertainty of any particular statement about animal minds, but on the applicability – the sense – of concepts employed in these statements. To insist that there must be psychological statements which are true of the lion, even though we cannot express them, is like insisting that it must be some time on the sun, even though we cannot tell it by our clocks.

Heroditus said that fire burns both in Hellas and in Persia but men's ideas of right and wrong vary from place to place. On this account, Heroditus did not take his relativism far enough. Wittgenstein's views about language, as applied to animal minds, represent the last turn of this relativist screw. The meaning of 'pain' is established only in a human context. And so, though fire burns in both the human and the cat world, only in the human world does it cause what we call 'pain'.

This situation is ironic. The Wittgensteinian view began by denying that the meaning of psychological terms could be established in a private context. It denies that I can only know what 'pain' means from my own case – semantic solipsism. But, *interpreted in this way*, it ends up by embracing a collective version of the same thesis – a kind of species solipsism or, if you prefer, semantic speciesism. In short, an anthropo*centric* conception of meaning is being offered as a reason for thinking that anthropo*morphism* is far more widespread than we habitually believe.

criticising the argument

This argument seems to establish a great deal; its problem is that, if it proves anything, it proves far too much. The argument moves from an account of the general conditions of communication and meaning to a conclusion about a particular set of concepts in a particular context, namely the application of psychological concepts to other animals. Concerning this it may be thought that:

1. The general theory of meaning invoked is wrong and so the conclusions concerning animals are wrong.

2. Whatever the truth of the general theory of meaning, its use in this context is a distraction from the real issues.

criticism I

First of all, it may be objected that this strategy simply runs the wrong way. We first legislate a general theory of meaning and then draw conclusions about what kinds of talk do and don't make sense. Shouldn't we do things the other way round? Shouldn't we look and see what kinds of talk do make sense and then construct our general theory upon such observations? And when we look at our talk about animals, what do we see? We see that we ascribe a large number of psychological states to animals and we are happy to do so.

picturing pain

To this reliance on our ordinary ways of talking, it may be replied that many such ascriptions are anthropomorphic. The whole point of applying a general theory of meaning to our talk about animals was to avoid the mythologies that can arise from anthropomorphism. We must come to accept that our concept, say, of cat pain, is mediated by the human experience and expression of pain, and by the characteristic structures of human life.

This sort of response can be reinforced by a more subtle point. Even those ascriptions which are not anthropomorphic cannot be regarded as straightforward accounts of animal experience. We must not depend on too simplistic a view about the ways in which concepts may be employed in a language. Not everything in language earns its place by doing the same job. In particular, not all linguistic terms work by simply and directly referring to classes of things in the world. At the limit, it is even possible to continue to use concepts in a language, though we do not have a clear grasp of their sense. And this, in fact, when we are not being anthropomorphic, is our position when we talk about the experience of animals.

An analogy may clarify the point. The French use the term 'sympathique' to refer to a particular quality of character. Notoriously, it is not translatable into English and, allegedly, the application of the concept cannot be mastered by non-French speakers. Nevertheless it is, in fact, used by English speakers. Yet, how, if they cannot understand what it means, can the English make use of it at all? It might be suggested that when used in English it refers not to the personality trait but to 'what it is that the French mean by "sympathique"'. We can only refer in English to the personality trait as it is represented in French. Because the English cannot use the word 'sympathique' to make discriminations in the real world, the word in English acts as a place holder for the discriminations that can be made only by the French in their own language – discriminations which the English know are possible but which they cannot make for themselves.

Similarly, it is suggested, when we talk of the cat being in pain, we do not, in our language, refer to the cat's pain. Our picture is not of the cat's pain but of 'whatever it is that the cat makes of its "pain"'. We can only refer to the cat's pain as it is represented in our language. The phrase 'the cat's pain' is a marker for an experience discriminable only by cats. It is a mistake to treat 'cat's pain' as referring to a particular fact in the world, which happens to be inaccessible to humans, rather than to a set of discriminations which cats do make and we do not. In confusing the fact of the cat's pain with what we are able to refer to, we reinforce the mythology of animal experience generated by common anthropomorphism.

In this kind of way, the appeal to our ordinary ways of talking about animals may be undermined by the critic who claims that

anthropomorphism is much more widespread than we usually suspect and who uses, in support, Wittgensteinian considerations about
meaning.

criticism II

What is wrong with deploying these considerations in this way is
that they prevent us from seeing where the real problem lies. If the
general conditions were really what mattered here, they would
constrain what it makes sense to say, not only about animal minds,
but about much else besides. If, *on these general grounds*, we are
prevented from making psychological ascriptions to animals, we
must also be forbidden from making other statements which are
unproblematic. The factors which are supposed to prevent us from
applying psychological concepts to animals ought also to prevent
us from applying psychological concepts to some members of the
human community. Infants, who are not yet linguistically compe-
tent, play no role in the conventions which fix the meanings of the
terms we use. Yet, we are reluctant to draw the conclusion that
statements about infant psychology are meaningless, rather than
just difficult to prove.

Worse still, nobody wants to deny that human language reaches
out to the physical world. Yet if we interpreted the general thesis in
the way in which it is applied to animals and applied it to the
physical world, we would arrive at conclusions that would strike us
as absurd. Ayers Rock and Alpha Centauri do not share in the
human conventions which govern the way in which we can refer to
mountains and stars. Yet, of course, this does not compromise our
ability to talk about such things, to make true and false statements
about them. The fact that our language is ours does not mean that
we cannot talk about things we have never encountered, places we
have never been, and times when we were not.

Human language does indeed depend upon human agreement
and ways of going on. And, properly understood, this does indeed
have implications for our understanding of animal minds. But, in
itself, the dependence of language on agreement and ways of going
on, does not restrict what we can agree about and the ways in which
we can go. In fact, the whole argument trades on mixing up
pre-conditions of meaningful discourse with the scope of the domains to which that discourse can be meaningfully applied. If I can
speak only English, then a condition of my speaking at all, is that I

speak in English. But it hardly follows that I can speak only about English things: cricket, crumpets and Stratford on Avon.

The absurdity of using the general argument to restrict the sphere of meaningful talk is, in these cases, apparent. And yet, when applied to animals, the use of the general argument seems much more plausible. 'The cat is on the mat' is a straightforward representation of a fact in the world, even though 'cat' and 'mat' and concepts of place are, of course, *our* concepts. Whereas it is plausible to suggest that there *is* a problem about 'the cat is in pain' which is connected with the concepts employed being our concepts. Somehow or other, it may strike us, the provenance of the concepts prevents such a statement from being a simple picture of the way things are.

Like 'mat', 'pain' is a human concept. Yet, unlike mats, pain is not a human artefact nor, most of us believe, does it only occur in human experience. And yet, the statement that employs the concept of pain can more plausibly be restricted to the human world. We have cause to worry that the fact that 'pain' is our concept somehow compromises straightforward claims about cats in pain. This is paradoxical. For according to the general considerations about meaning allegedly derived from Wittgenstein, this is the opposite of what one should expect.

This suggests that what is causing the problem is not something to do with communication in general, but the particular features of psychological concepts. This becomes obvious when we contrast 'the cat is on the mat' with 'the cat sees the mat'. The introduction of a concept of perception makes us query in what sense it is a *mat* that is being seen.

But why should psychological concepts be compromised by the fact that they are ours when many other kinds of concepts are not compromised for this reason?

In fact, the thought that these concepts are our concepts is a red herring. It makes it seem as if the underlying truth is species relativism. It is not that they are *our* psychological concepts but that they are our *psychological* concepts. The real work is being done not by the fact that psychological concepts are our concepts (and hence can't apply elsewhere) but by the fact that in applying psychological concepts, we attribute concept use to those creatures and we do not know what these concepts can be. It is not that these concepts only belong to us; it is that we cannot see how they could, as we think they must, belong to them. We must examine this topic in the next chapter.

summary

We have seen that anthropomorphism is not a single, simple error. It is itself complex with different forms, many of which are benign and only some of which are likely to lead to serious intellectual error. The most glaring examples are the least damaging; the old lady who gossips with her budgerigar is not a threat to scientific understanding. The examples of anthropomorphism which are alleged to be the most dangerous are also those which remain the most controversial.

This is because anti-anthropomorphism is not a methodology but a goal. It is not a means of carrying out animal research but one characteristic of a successful outcome. If it is anthropomorphic to speak of whales and their language of song, then indeed some current cetaceous research is losing itself in a world of intellectual error and confusion. On the other hand, if whales really have what it makes sense to call a language, then to call it so will not be anthropomorphic. The trouble is that it has yet to be shown that talking about the language of whales is or isn't anthropomorphic. A general prohibition against anthropomorphism does not decide the issue one way or another. Inveighing against anthropomorphism is no more part of scientific methodology than exhortations to score goals are part of the tactics of soccer.

People who are generally suspicious of claims that we can understand other animal minds are too ready to trace any and all problems to anthropomorphism. This is because anthropomorphism has come to be treated as a generic term, a catch-all, for every difficulty that we encounter when we try to understand minds different from our own. But, as we have seen, anthropomorphism is not any kind of mis-ascription but one of a particular kind. It means *inappropriately* thinking of what is not human in terms that apply to humans. The trouble with treating anthropomorphism as a generic mistake, is that we are less likely to see what other kinds of failure are possible. 'Anthropomorphic' is not the opposite of 'scientific': there are more ways of being wrong about animals than being anthropomorphic. A further consequence of the preoccupation with anthropomorphism is that because there is only one criterion of failure in the animal sciences, there is only one criterion of success: that the methodologies for understanding animal experience should match, as closely as possible, the methodologies for understanding physical objects. Researchers remain loyal to a single methodology even if the actual results are disappointing and banal. Opportunities for opening up the animal world through new methodologies are overlooked or denigrated.

Scientists are correct to be wary of anthropomorphism because it leads to overindulgence in psychological ascriptions. But the fear of anthropomorphism can lead to a kind of ascriptive anorexia. Overindulgence can lead to sentimentalism and, in the animal sciences, to florid and undisciplined speculation. But anorexia, even if it produces lean science, reinforces, in our wider relations with animals, the prevailing culture of denial. It is therefore an open question whether, either within the animal sciences or in our culture at large, ascriptive overindulgence or ascriptive anorexia is the bigger threat.

What, we hope, can be agreed is that arming ourselves against anthropomorphism cannot amount to solving all problems about the understanding of minds other than our own.

We have also argued that recent attempts by philosophers to show that anthropomorphism is much more pervasive that we think are mistaken. In particular, attempts to show that anthropomorphism arises naturally from widespread but naive conceptions of the nature of human language fail. The fact that our language is *ours* does not in itself mean that all our talk about the non-human is systematically corrupt. What is true is that there is something puzzling about the nature of psychological ascriptions which has to be taken seriously if our investigation is to advance. To this problem, how it is that we can ascribe psychological concepts to non-language using creatures, we must now turn.

notes

1. *Against Liberation: Putting Animals in Perspective* by Michael Leahey (London, Routledge, 1991). Leahey's book attempts to show that anthropomorphism is much more widespread than we think using arguments which, the author believes, derive from the philosophy of Wittgenstein.

2. See *Tractatus Logico-Philosophicus* by Ludwig Wittgenstein

(Routledge and Kegan Paul, London, 1961). Ludwig Wittgenstein (1889-1951) was an Austrian philosopher who for most of his life lived and worked in Cambridge. He was a deeply spiritual, though eccentric man who twice overturned the fundamental philosophical ideas of his time. The *Tractatus* was published in 1921 and influenced an entire generation of philosophers. It is a short, enigmatic and strangely beautiful work which deals with fundamental themes in the philosophy of logic and ethics. Derek Jarman's recent film *Wittgenstein* (1993) is a entertaining way for the beginner to start exploring his life and ideas.

3. *Philosophical Investigations* by Ludwig Wittgenstein (Basil Blackwell, Oxford, 1958) S. 351. This posthumous work, published in 1953, consists of 693 numbered remarks with additional material, covering an enormous range of themes but focusing on the nature of meaning and mind. Amongst many other things, the book is a painstaking and comprehensive analysis of the philosophy of the earlier *Tractatus*. It tries to explain how his earlier misconceptions about language and mind are deep illusions to which we are always prone. It is considered by many to be the most important philosophical work of the 20th century.

4. See *Philosophical Investigations* by Ludwig Wittgenstein (Basil Blackwell, Oxford, 1958) S. 38.

6: the speechless lion

'Perhaps I could know what a lion is thinking, but only if it could tell me. Unfortunately, I can't talk to lions.'
This suggests that the real obstacle to understanding animal minds is that animals do not talk. If they did, we would have no more problem in understanding them than we have in understanding other human beings from different cultures. We could come to see the world through their eyes and achieve real insight into the ways in which they experience their worlds. This was the dream of Dr Dolittle.

Unfortunately this dream is a fantasy. The question of linguistic communication does not arise in relation to the vast majority of species. Even the most promising cases remain problematic and highly controversial. Consequently all that richness is locked behind silence.

This is a tempting analysis of the way things are. Understanding what is wrong with it and what is right about it forms the topic of this chapter.

Here is a very different account of the issue. Wittgenstein writes:

If a lion could talk, we could not understand him.[1]

If Dr Dolittle heard this he would be speechless. He would consider that the philosophy of Wittgenstein arms an aggressive scepticism about animal minds. Like a number of thinkers, he would accuse Wittgenstein of being a species chauvinist because he insists that the meaning of all our concepts and, in particular, of our psychological concepts, are limited to the human domain.

How could it be true, Dolittle might ask, that we *could* not understand a talking lion? It might be difficult; perhaps as a matter of fact it would be beyond our ingenuity. But what entitles us to rule out the possibility from the start? What obstacle stands in our way that could not be overcome? What marks out leonine speech from cuneiform tablets?

Unravelling its meaning requires patience but Wittgenstein's ten-word epigram turns out to illuminate a nest of problems associated with the Dolittle ambition.

Like many philosophical suppositions, the epigram asks us on the one hand to take the possibility envisaged seriously, and on the other, to ignore much of what would also have to be true if such a possibility were to be realised. This may seem perverse but is often how philosophical thought-experiments have to be. So we really are to suppose that the lion can speak and therefore to ignore the plain fact that lions can't talk. And we are further required to ignore what may be true: that the acquisition of language would transform leonine experience into something else – we are to suppose that the lion remains a lion.

Further, the rhetorical force of the remark depends on the expectation that the reader, no matter what his experience of lions, will reject the conclusion. So, Wittgenstein asks us to assume, in the funny way proper to philosophical thought experiments, that:

- we know all there is to know about the psychological states of the lion;

- the lion can really speak;

- the lion remains in all other regards a lion.

He then concludes that still we could not understand him.

Why not? Wittgenstein wants us to question the natural thought that because we already know a lot about what the lion cares about, we know what he would talk about and roughly how he would talk, if he could speak. Contrary to this common assumption, Wittgenstein argues that the way the world must be talked about cannot be read off from the world, not even from facts about the likes and dislikes of those who do the talking. It is always mediated by the activities of language-users and these, from any external perspective, are inherently unpredictable. On this reading, the epigram is a claim about language and meaning, in particular, about the relation of concepts to reality.

As an analogy, consider the claim that there has to be a basis, physiological and psychological, for the games that humans play. It is possible for soccer to be a human game only because we have the sorts of bodies and the sorts of experience we have. This means, among other things, that if humans had fins instead of legs they could not play soccer. And, arguing in retrospect, soccer looks like a very appropriate game for legged animals like us to develop. But neither of these claims means that the rules of soccer can be derived from physiology or psychology; nor that the normativity of the rules and the concepts they employ can be derived from physical necessities. The 'mustn'ts' of the rules cannot be derived from the 'cannots' of the laws.

So what Wittgenstein was saying in epigrammatic form was this:

> If a lion could speak we could not understand him because there is no way we can read off from the lion's experience, however much we know about it, how the lion would incorporate language into its life. One cannot infer from natural facts about the lion's experience or behaviour the conventions that would constitute the language games of the lion.

determining sense

If Wittgenstein is right, then lurking beneath the charming fantasy of Dr Dolittle, there is a fundamental philosophical problem about our understanding of animal minds. There is a real difficulty in trying to understand a lion's experience, but not because lions do not speak. The problem is there in the case of ordinary lions too. What we cannot do, just by looking at lions, is to determine the content of the animal's perspective on the world. We need to examine this idea in more detail.

We have seen that most of us most of the time are ready to make all sorts of ascriptions of psychological states to many other kinds of animals. We say such things as the lion notices the antelope, the wolf is keeping an eye on its rivals, the dog has gone outside to fetch its bone. When we make such attributions, we are attributing to the animal a psychological state with a particular content. It is this content that marks out the particular state that the animal is in from any other. How is the content of this psychological state fixed? The content of this state is given in the concepts we employ in the attribution for example, 'antelope', 'rival' and 'bone'. What this means is that in attributing the state to the animal, we are also attributing *the use* of the concepts 'antelope', 'rival' or 'bone'. There are two problems about the attribution of such concepts.

The first problem should be familiar. Concepts such as 'antelope', 'rival' and 'bone' are clearly human concepts. How can we ever know that it is these concepts that fix the particular content of the animal's psychological states? This, of course, is the worry about anthropomorphism that we discussed in the last chapter. The second problem, though connected, is nevertheless sufficiently disquieting to be discussed separately. The philosopher Donald Davidson provides a useful summary:

..without speech we cannot make the fine distinctions between thoughts that are essential to the explanations which we can sometimes confidently supply...the intentionality we make so much of in the attribution of thoughts is very hard to make much of when speech is not present. The dog, we say, knows that its master is home. But does it know that Mr Smith (who is his master), or that the President of the Bank (who is that same master), is home? We have no real idea of how to settle, or how to make sense, of these questions.[2]

The fundamental idea is that if it is to make sense to say that a creature has psychological states, it must be possible for these states to be distinguished one from another. If a creature possesses psychological states, they must be particular ones. Some kinds of states, especially sensations, may be distinguished from one another by how they feel; by what it is like for the creature to have them; what is sometimes called the 'qualia' of an experience. But other kinds of psychological states cannot be distinguished one from another on the basis of qualia alone. For example, different beliefs cannot be distinguished on the grounds of what it feels like to have them. The belief that Disraeli was the greatest Victorian Prime Minister is different from the belief that Gladstone was. But the difference cannot consist in what it feels like to hold one belief rather than another.

Most of us do want to attribute more than sensations to animals. We want to explain an animal's behaviour by talking about its *cognitive* relation to its world. It behaves as it does because it is in a psychological state with a particular content – a content that is connected with *how the world is* for the animal. In these cases, where we are attributing the use of concepts to the animal, what it is like to be in this state will not help to give the psychological state its distinctive identity. If an animal fears that a predator will attack its young, what it fears cannot be determined by the experience of fear. How it feels to be frightened cannot determine the content of the fear – that it is this predator and these cubs that are the object of the animal's anxious attention. On the contrary, the character of fear is conditioned by its object.

A widely supported conclusion in modern philosophy is that in our case, beliefs and thoughts can be about one thing rather than another because they are enlanguaged. A thought is nothing other than the representation of the world as being in some particular state. We can say what a particular thought is by saying what the thought says about how the world is. Thus in the statement 'Bill Clinton believes that Al Gore is a good Vice-President', what picks out Clinton's thought as this particular one is what is represented by the linguistic clause that comes after 'that'. On this view, in the human case, and we must suppose, in the case of language-users generally, we identify thoughts by using language to pick out the actual or possible state of affairs which the thought is about.

How can we be sure that a thought really does pick out some actual or possible state of affairs and so really is different from other thoughts that might have occurred? One answer given by contemporary philosophers is that we can ensure this by insisting that the thought be capable of being true or false. There must be some particular state of affairs which would make it true or false. And being 'aimed' at this particular state of affairs is what makes the thought distinctive from any other. In our case, it makes sense for us to attribute thoughts to each other because we can specify precisely the content of the attributed thoughts by linguistically pointing at the actual or possible state of affairs which the thought is about – the state of affairs which, if actual, would make the thought true. In short, in our case, the medium of language allows our beliefs, thoughts and other cognitive states to have a definite content, a determinate sense.

But now we face the question: what, in the case of non-language using animals, does the job that language does for us? That is, what is it that makes it possible for an animal's psychological state to be 'about' some particular thing in the world? What is it that makes the lion's 'noticing', the noticing of that antelope rather than the noticing of a meal or of a moving object? In short, what gives animal thoughts a determinate sense? The difficulty of answering this question may lead us to dismiss out of hand the kind of analysis of animal behaviour that some anti-behaviourist animal scientists wish to give.

Donald Griffin, for example, complains that the strange behaviour of nesting plovers when threatened by predators is often explained by scientists in terms of an incoherent behavioural pattern, caused by the clash between the need for flight and the need to fight. Sometimes, according to Griffin, the elaborate pattern of abnormal gait, broken-wing display, squatting in the sand as if incubating, movement towards and then away from the predator, is at least recognised by scientists as an elaborate and effective piece of predator-distraction. But even then, what the plover does is explained by animal scientists as being nothing more than automatic reflex behaviour created by natural selection. The proximate cause of the behaviour is simply identified with its evolutionary function. The question of the significance of the threat and the response for the animal is either ignored or considered senseless. Griffin writes:

> If we pull ourselves out of this negative dogmatism, we can begin to ask what birds engaged in predator-distraction behavior might be feeling and thinking....

> ...The bird might...think about two possibilities: either [the intruder] will come to my young and hurt them, or it will go off in some other direction and leave them alone. If the bird considers these two possibilities, it will obviously prefer the second. As it slowly stands up and walks away, it might think, 'I can make that intruder go away from my young.' The display of false incubation fits into this simple expectation. 'If that creature comes closer, it may see me rather than my youngsters.'[3]

For many in the animal sciences, this kind of approach is simply beyond the pale. But even if we are sympathetic to Griffin's attack on Behaviourism, we are still left with the philosophical problem of what it can be about the plover that gives its thoughts this particular sense.

It should be clear that the problem is not that in attributing psychological states to animals, we are using human concepts rather than leonine or canine concepts. After all, as we saw earlier (see p. 101), something analogous to this occurs when we attribute thoughts to other humans who speak a language which is not easily translatable to our own. In such cases, we are sure that, whatever the difficulties of our specifying the other's thought, the thought is perfectly definite and determinate for them. But in the case of other animals, we have a problem over and above the difficulty of translation. The question of how non-language using creatures can have the determinate states that we ascribe to them can be raised independently of whether *we* can know that they are in such states or understand what they are.

Nor is the problem the one we noted earlier (see p. 75) concerning the nature of reflective self-consciousness and its connection with 'simple' consciousness. That problem concerned the relative logical priority of 'simple', first-order beliefs and 'reflective', second-order beliefs. Can a creature have beliefs at all if it is incapable of believing that it has beliefs? But this question is irrelevant if it does not make sense to ascribe any beliefs to a non-language user because such beliefs could not have any content.

One response to the difficulties about determinacy of sense is that we are simply wrong to ascribe states with determinate content to animals. The contemporary consensus about the intimate relation between language and thought is correct and, more or less, complete. Thoughts require determinate content. Determinate content is available only through the articulate structures of a language. Hence non-language using creatures are not capable of thought.

We should be clear what this amounts to. It does not merely mean, what all of us believe already, that cats do not make very innovative physicists; that octopuses do not ponder the dilemmas of the solitary life; that working sheep dogs do not spend their idle moments contemplating the problems of modern agricultural practice. The argument that thoughts cannot have a determinate content without language does not apply only to very complicated, highly general or, for that matter, highly particular thoughts. If its conclusion is true, it is true of thought as such, even what we describe as primitive or unsophisticated cognitive responses to the world. It means that our common belief that domestic, working and wild animals find their way through their worlds by observing, noticing and discovering what is going on must be an illusion. But if so, it is an illusion that animals have minds. For all the world, the dog searching for its buried bone certainly looks like the human being searching for the buried drain. But, really, in one case there is someone searching. In the other, there is only the searching. Dr Dolittle's ambition is a fantasy not because we cannot *talk* to animals but because there is no one to talk *to*.

the dilemma

What are we to make of this? We face a dilemma. Most of us, most of the time are perfectly comfortable making psychological attributions to animals that implicitly and explicitly involve the attribution of concept use to them. These attributions seem natural, useful and inevitable. On the other hand, there are powerful arguments, deeply engrained in contemporary philosophy, which insist that because of the intimate connections between thought, concept-use and language, it does not make sense to make such attributions. What are we to believe?

Three strategies for dealing with this dilemma present themselves:

- We can cast our lot in with contemporary philosophy. The tie-up between language and thought has proved fruitful in many areas of philosophy. This does mean that a great deal of our ordinary talk about animals will prove to be systematically defective. It should be admitted that this is disquieting. After all, the philosophers who did the most to convince us that language and thought are woven together were also of the view that it was a mistake to hold that whole tracts of our ordinary ways of speaking could be systematically defective. Precisely because language and thought run together, they argued that it does not make sense to stand outside our linguistic practices and ask whether or not they correspond to reality. In this case, we are dealing with the relationship of our ordinary talk to the reality of animals. Still, we must bite the bullet. If psychological states are to have content, they must be the psychological states of language-using creatures. Perhaps we can improve matters by trying to understand why we are so peculiarly prone to illusion about other animals. Perhaps, as Kennedy[4] suggests, such an illusion is driven by evolutionary pressures.

Language-using creatures who are really capable of forming beliefs and thoughts about the world do better if they treat the non-language using creatures they encounter as if they too had these states.

- We can remain loyal to our ordinary talk about animals. We do ascribe psychological states to animals. Contemporary philosophy must then simply be wrong to insist on such a close connection between language and thought. It is true that no account of what it is for psychological states to have content immediately presents itself. But we must not rest content with a solution to this problem which we know to be false.

- We can seek to reduce the tension between the philosophical view about language and thought and the validity of our ordinary talk. Here there are a number of tactical options which we need to explore.

reducing the tension

We might hold that contemporary philosophy is right to insist that psychological states must meet the requirement for determinacy of sense. But, we might go on, this is not the reason our ordinary explanations of animal behaviour are suspect. The reason our ordinary talk is suspect is that we habitually exaggerate the variety and the extent of those aspects of *human* capacities and activities which require explanation in terms of psychological states with complex content. Much more of our own behaviour can be explained in terms of mechanisms which have no more need to refer to anything in the world than a thermostat needs to have a concept of temperature. Rather they come into play automatically, triggered by internal processes or external stimuli. Consequently, there is much less of a gulf between the kinds of explanation that we need for animal behaviour and the kinds we need for our own. Our natural explanations of animal behaviour *are* defective but only because our natural explanations of our own are defective. 'Folk Psychology' – the supposed theory of ourselves that underlies our ordinary talk about each other – is no better than our unsophisticated 'Critter Psychology'.

That is one possibility. Alternatively, we might hold that contemporary philosophy is right to insist that psychological states meet the requirement for determinacy of sense. But it is wrong to believe that only language can enable thought to meet this requirement. As the young Wittgenstein believed (see p. 95) language is only one kind of representation. And it is the power of representational structures which enables language to do its job. So what enables psychological states to be about anything are representational structures. As we saw earlier (see p. 82), it may be claimed that such representations need not have all the complexity of the things in the world that they represent. They need only have sufficient complexity to enable a creature to survive. Perhaps, if we understood how these representational structures work, we would see that they could be identified with neurophysiological functions embedded in neural structures common to us and other animals. We might then see that the determinacy of the content of animal beliefs can be explained in terms of the specificity of the underlying neural mechanism.

Both these responses are essentially empiricist in character. But it is possible to see the outline of a non-empiricist response to the dilemma, one that is consistent with taking animal minds seriously.

the illusion of super-rigid meaning

How might this view be developed? We might hold that while there is something right about the connection between language and thought made by contemporary philosophy, the connection is one that holds only when we remain within our point of view. And that point of view is inherently linguistic.

The result is that we put far too high a premium on an *objective* requirement for determinacy of sense. Most of the time, within our linguistic communities and practices, our thought and talk unambiguously pick out states of affairs in the world. But we conclude, invalidly, that the same connections would be seen to hold if we were able to view ourselves objectively, from outside our linguistic activities. As it were, if God could look into our minds, He would see what we were thinking or talking about.[5] Now it seems to us that words, and hence our thoughts, pick out items in the world with a kind of super-precision. The super-hard, *objective* determinacy of our concepts excludes all possibility of ambiguity and hence of misunderstanding. The meaning of what we think and say is like a perfect arrow which points unerringly at its target. And this is what explains the fact that, most of the time, we manage to make sense of one another. The coherence of our language and our thought is guaranteed by an inherent harmony between the structure of language and the structure of the world we describe, which is independent of our actual linguistic practices.

It is significant that Wittgenstein, who is widely thought to have insisted on the connection between language and thought, also tried to undermine this picture of the perfect, objective, determinacy of the meaning of the terms we use. He wrote:

> A picture is conjured up which seems to fix the sense unambiguously. The actual use, compared with that suggested by the picture, seems like something muddied...the form of expression we use seems to have been designed for a god....
>
> In the actual use of expressions we make detours, we go by side-roads. We see the straight highway before us, but of course we cannot use it, because it is permanently closed.[6]

In emphasising the importance of the actual use of expressions, Wittgenstein was not trying to present a rival negative picture of language as inherently vague and ambiguous. Rather he was seeking to present a positive but subtle position: the source of the sense of our words and thoughts – how the arrow succeeds in pointing – lies within, and only within, our linguistic practice:

> How does it come about that this arrow ➜ points? Doesn't it seem to carry in it something beside itself? – 'No, not the dead line on paper; only the psychical thing, the meaning, can do that.' – That is both true and false. The arrow points only in the application that a living being makes of it.
>
> This pointing is not a hocus-pocus which can be performed only by the soul.
>
> We want to say: 'When we mean something, it's like going up to someone. it's not having a dead picture (of any kind).' We go up to the thing we mean.
>
> Yes: meaning something is like going up to someone.[7]

In this passage, Wittgenstein presents us with a three-way exchange between himself, an advocate of a non-empiricist or 'mentalist' account of meaning and, in the background, an advocate of an empiricist theory of meaning. Wittgenstein agrees with the empiricist that meaning is not some non-natural phenomenon ('a hocus-pocus') which could be carried out only by a supernatural soul. But he disagrees that it could be produced merely by a representation, even a neural one ('a dead picture [of any kind]').

His non-empiricist or mentalist opponent believes that words and thoughts magically reach out to the things to which they refer *as if* they were going up to someone to shake his hand or kiss him on the cheek. Wittgenstein agrees with this opponent that meaning something *is* like going up to someone. But, he suggests, this is not true, as his opponent intends, in a merely metaphorical sense. Rather, our meaning something *really* is like going up to someone. Meaning gets going because we move around and act upon a world of other objects and agents. Meaning is no less natural and no more mysterious than the kinds of activities in which living beings engage.

Wittgenstein's point here is that the sense of our thoughts and words is not rooted in any objective connection between terms and the world which might be inspected from outside our linguistic practices and checked for its rigidity. The meaning of the concepts we use is not something fixed independently of the use to which these concepts are put inside human life with all its contingencies. Our concepts do not have a super-hard determinacy so that, for all possible situations, it can be decided whether or not expressions that describe them are true or false. Rather our words, our concepts and our thoughts have no more, but no less determinacy than the forms of living practice in which they are embedded.

For Wittgenstein, meaning is not a supernatural phenomenon nor a material, causal phenomenon. But it is a natural one. A natural, *anthropological* phenomenon.

meaning as insider-dealing

What this means is that the meaning of a term or the content of a concept is not something which is visible from a perspective external to that of the community of practice, in which the terms and concepts are embedded. From inside the community, no inherent defects in the determinacy of a concept are visible. Its members go on as they do. Within those uses, the determinacy seems complete because questions which, from an external point of view it might be possible to ask, do not arise. On the Wittgensteinian view, meaning and its relative determinacy, is a matter of insider-dealing.

This does not necessarily mean that the internal perspective of the community must remain forever closed to outside observers. Anthropologists are skilled at the delicate task of hopping to and fro across the borders of human communities, becoming sufficiently involved within the community to grasp how things are from there and yet sufficiently detached to avoid being absorbed by it, so that their accounts may yet be understood by members of different communities. Anthropology is an inherently problematic inquiry but it is not impossible. It is only that anthropologists must remember that questions which can be asked and given definite answers in a particular culture may be senseless when asked about other cultures. The question 'Is this practice magic or primitive science?', which has a determinate sense within our culture, may be unanswerable when asked of another. It cuts across the grain of their practices. But that does not mean that there is anything indeterminate or suspect about the concepts of that culture or of ours.

This account of the nature of meaning is of direct relevance to the dilemma concerning our attribution of concept possession to animals. Such an account inoculates us against a kind of subtle and profound anthropomorphism to which crusaders against more obvious forms of anthropomorphism are especially prone.

The anthropomorphic error occurs when it is claimed that animals cannot be thought to be users of concepts because there is no evidence that, say, a dog distinguishes between 'bones', 'toys' and 'food'. Even if we knew everything there was to know about the dog's behaviour, it may be claimed, we should still not be able to determine which of these concepts were possessed by the animal. The logical shadow cast by the animal's behaviour is so lacking in shape that it cannot be called a concept at all. Hence, it does not make sense to say that the animal has these or any other concepts.

But insisting that the question like 'Does the dog think its master is a top dog or not a dog at all?', because it is a well-formed question in English, must have an answer in terms of what is going on in the dog, is anthropomorphic. Language-users are able to ask questions, the answers to which cannot be found in the lives of non-language-users. But not because the non-language-users lack something. A dog's beliefs about the location of its bone are perfectly in order. There need be no vagueness or imprecision about them. Vagueness, imprecision, misapprehension and uncertainty may all occur in a dog's life as they do in ours. But they are not linguistic vagueness or semantic imprecision and their uncertainties do not emerge in the form of questions about the truth values of beliefs. It does not mean that we cannot ascribe to animals psychological states which have a distinctive cognitive content.

The point is not just that, in language, humans are able to form concepts which seem to them inevitable ways of describing the world, but to which nothing need correspond in the life of other animals. Language confers on our view of the world structural features, the possession of which transforms our experience of it; structures which allow us to ask particular kinds of question about the content of what we think and say. We can ask 'What does such and such mean?' and answers in terms of increasingly accurate definitions are always available. This capacity, which is characteristic only of language-users, sets up an ideal of determinate, precise meaning, an ideal to which, it seems, all thought and belief must conform. Once we are enmeshed in language, all meaning looks like this kind of linguistic meaning. This foists on us the illusion that meaning must always be the perfectly focused photograph, always capable of revealing more and more detail on closer inspection. When we ask about the content of animal concepts and find that no precise answers are available, we are left with the disturbing thought that the animal's head is filled with fuzzy snapshots. Or we conclude that no picture so vague could really be a picture of anything at all and so there can be no pictures in the animal's head. If we are already committed to the false idea that to use a concept is to have something akin to a picture in one's head then we must conclude that animals do not possess concepts.

To think that this is a reason for withholding our ascriptions is a species of anthropomorphism. One that might appropriately be called *logomorphism* – the fallacy of thinking of what is not a language-user in terms that apply only to language-users. Instead, we should be more careful in our treatment of the determinacy of animal thought. We should not demand linguistic specificity of non-language-users and we should not commit ourselves in advance to the thesis that the kind of determinacy that linguistic thought has is the only kind of determinacy possible. But how else can it be conceived?

We have said that Wittgenstein understands human meaning and concept-possession as a natural, anthropological phenomenon. What this suggests is the possibility of a parallel account for animals, one that will offer at least the shape of an answer to Davidson's puzzlement about the content of the canine concept of master. We must understand animal meaning and concept possession as an *ethological* phenomenon.

conclusion

Still, having accepted the strictures against logomorphism, we cannot simply ignore the problem of determinacy of sense. If animals have the psychological states that we ascribe to them, then those states must have content, and so there must be something to differentiate one such state from another. So, what we need to identify are those features or aspects of animal lives that provide that content. This is not to say that an understanding of animal meaning and concept possession as an *ethological* phenomenon will hold that the animal mind is as specific as its behaviour. Putting the point this way gives the misleading impression that animal minds are nothing but patterns of behaviour and we hope that we have already exposed Behaviourism as a metaphysical muddle. Rather, we need to conceive of the way in which the animal mind is as specific as its life. A life which is constituted by the *possibilities* of behaviour that are open to it within its species nature. In this, we think one concept is crucial: the concept of *expression*.

The foundations and prospects of such an approach, the implications for the methodologies of the animal sciences, as well as some of the further barriers that need to be overcome, we shall examine in subsequent chapters.

notes

1. *Philosophical Investigations* by Ludwig Wittgenstein (Basil Blackwell, Oxford, 1958) S. 223.

2. 'Thought and talk' by Donald Davidson in *Inquiries into Truth and Interpretation* (The Clarendon Press, Oxford, 1984). The author is an American philosopher whose work has greatly influenced the modern generation of philosophers.

3. *Animal Thinking* by Donald R. Griffin (Harvard University Press, Cambridge, 1984), p. 93.

4. *The New Anthropomorphism* by J.S. Kennedy (Cambridge University Press, 1992).

5. C.f. *Philosophical Investigations* by Ludwig Wittgenstein (Basil Blackwell, Oxford, 1958), p. 217.

6. *Philosophical Investigations* by Ludwig Wittgenstein (Basil Blackwell, Oxford, 1958) S. 426.

7. *Philosophical Investigations* by Ludwig Wittgenstein (Basil Blackwell, Oxford, 1958) SS. 454, 455, 457.

7: the experienced world

Is it possible to understand the experience of creatures other than ourselves? One way in which to support the view that it *is*, is to argue that *all* experience must exhibit certain properties. If all experience *must* have certain properties and if we could discover what they are, then we would know of any creature that its experience must have these properties. We would be forced to acknowledge that human experience is only one of the ways in which these properties can be realised. We would understand our experience as just an instance of the general principles governing all experience.

In this chapter, we shall explore the issues surrounding this approach to the problem of animal minds.

What could possibly justify the claim that it is possible to know something about the character of all experience? Isn't the character of experience precisely that which is accidental and unpredictable?

the limits of experience

The character of experience arises from the interaction between the kind of environment in which a creature lives and the kind of sensory and neurological physiology which it has evolved. It may be thought that since there are no limits to the variety of environments or to the variety of physiology – no limits to possible worlds and the types of creature that inhabit them – there is no theoretical limit to the variety of possible experience. There is nothing which is true of all experience.

However, it is possible to make two distinct kinds of objection, one practical and one theoretical, to the idea that there is no limit to possible experience.

the practical approach

The first objection insists that we do know quite a lot both about the environments in which creatures evolve specific physiologies and about the mechanisms which drive that evolution. Not any old physical conditions will prove suitable for the evolution of a creature. Not any environment can be a habitat. Whole environments are inimical to life. Most scientists agree that it is impossible for life to exist either on Venus (roughly because it is too hot) or on Neptune (roughly because it is too cold). Only within a narrow band of possible planetary environments can life develop and thrive. For this reason, we should not expect the variety of experience to increase proportionally to the variety of environments.

A second practical objection is that the Theory of Natural Selection tells us to expect that, within a particular environment, specific sensory and neurological mechanisms will exist precisely because they represent the best available fit between the animal's evolutionary history and the more or less recent character of its environment. So whereas in the contrived world of fashion there is no limit to variety in, for example, the design of men's ties, in the severe economy of Nature, the rich variety of life should not obscure the fact that future possibilities are constrained by evolutionary history.

Of course, particular ecological niches may result in adaptive strategies issuing in unexpected kinds of experience. The bat teaches us that increased retinal sensitivity is not the only solution to having to make one's living at night; electric eels and dolphins teach us that we should be careful not to discount unthinkingly features of the world, such as voltage gradients, as irrelevant to animals of roughly this size; homing pigeons that global effects, like the magnetic field of the earth, can be used to find one's way around. But these variations cluster around the central core of types of experience with which we are familiar.

Perhaps such a tale could be told about cognitive as well as sensory experience. For again, the evolution of such systems must be driven by the mechanisms of natural selection as they grip the track of how the world really is. Thus what matters, at the scale of things where there are sentient creatures, are not strange sub-atomic indeterminacies, but the smoothed out behaviour of middle-sized conglomerations of atoms – what we call 'objects'. Thus we would expect that cognitive systems have mechanisms for identifying such objects, tracking them and manipulating them in time and space. This requires at least some minimal means of representing how things are in the world, what we can call 'beliefs', and at least some minimal means of tracking objects over time, what we can call 'memory'. It is in this kind of way that we might try to develop an account of a more or less coherent core of cognitive mechanisms, embedded in physiological structures gradually evolved by the process of adaptive selection.

but what about experience itself?

Perhaps we should not be impressed by arguments of this sort. Maybe a crucial step in the argument is flawed. Creatures do need to be able to respond to the dominant features of the world in which they find themselves. It is to be expected, for example, that the development of eyes should be a runaway selective success. But does it follow that if creatures have visual systems with similar functions, they must have similar *visual experiences*? Why are we so confident that sensory systems which are sensitive to certain wavelengths of light all produce experience which is anything like what we call visual experience? Even putting aside creatures with photo-sensitive skin, do mechanisms which are responsive to light in the ways that eyes are, have to produce a way the world *looks*?

If we ask 'Does the Theory of Natural Selection provide any empirical reason for believing that experience must have a particular content and shape?' there are two possible answers. If experience is a by-product of the way that natural selection moulds functional systems, then the answer is 'No': experience will be essentially open-ended. If, on the other hand, natural selection, on its way to moulding functional systems, must go *through* the character of experience, the answer will be 'Yes': what experiences are possible *will* be limited by whatever factors are the effective determinants within the natural economy.

Figure 7.1 (see over) represents the view that experience is a collateral effect of the development of physiological systems. For example, mechanisms which are responsive to light, produce, at least in some animals, something that we call a way the world 'looks', but the character of visual experience is functionally sterile. From the point of view of evolution, the character of experience is *epiphenomenal*: that is, though the experience is produced causally

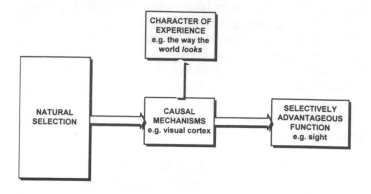

Fig. 7.1 Experience and natural selection – the negative view.

by underlying physical mechanisms, it does not in itself produce any selective advantage. The selective advantage consists in producing physiological systems with a determinate function, not in being a creature whose experiences have a particular content and shape. This may seem a natural consequence of the view that natural selection operates neither on species nor on particular animals but on patterns of genetic material. If natural selection operates on genes and genes do not have types of experience, then natural selection cannot operate on types of experiences. This accounts for the fact that, for example, in the world of bacteria we find functional sophistication with what most of us believe to be an absence of experience. Whereas, in the human world, rich experiences, like listening to Bruckner and doing theoretical physics, have no direct functional significance whatsoever.

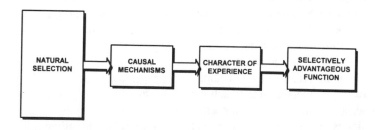

Fig. 7.2 Experience and natural selection – the positive view.

The alternative view (see Fig. 7.2) is that, if natural selection 'aims' at producing particular functions, it must at the same time select for the appropriate kinds of experiences – the kinds of experience which, as a matter of fact, are required if that particular function is to be realised. So, being able to see things is the way in which the function of movement through the world *via* the reflective surfaces of objects is realised. Whatever it is like to have echo-location, it is part and parcel of being able to find one's way *via* the propensity of objects to reflect sound. Within the machinery of selection, experience is not an idle wheel.

Adopting this view does not mean embracing Lamarckism (see p. 20). It means refusing to enlist in evolutionary epiphenomenalism. Like other kinds of epiphenomenalism, the evolutionary variety entails that Nature expends its efforts on the production of phenomena, experiences of all kinds, which are essentially idle. It also sets *a priori* limits to the explanatory power of one of our most successful scientific theories. If experience is outside the purview of the Theory of Natural Selection, then since experience is not some miracle but part of the biological world, the theory must be inadequate.

According to this line of argument, the reach of the Theory of Natural Selection ought not to be curtailed prematurely. Its scope includes kinds of experience because experience is relevant to the functional significance of behaviour. Therefore, kinds of experience *do* correlate with kinds of sensory systems. So, for example, sensory systems sensitive to light are useful. But more than that, they are useful, at least to most creatures, precisely because they produce a way the world looks. So the Theory of Natural Selection does give us reason to believe that we can know something of the experience of other creatures. If a creature has well-developed eyes, then we can know that it *sees*.

Arguments like these lead to the conclusion that the more we understand Nature, the more we can understand what experience must be. The upshot is that scepticism about our ability to understand animal minds is unscientific.

the theoretical approach

In contrast, the second kind of response to the claim that there are no limits to kinds of experience is a theoretical, *a priori* one. It proceeds not from particular facts about how the world is but from trying to analyse the concept of experience. Its starting point is the thought that not everything we can imagine strikes us as a possible kind of experience. That is, it is possible to make claims about what experience might be which strike us as ridiculous or nonsensical – claims which fail to make sense because they conflict with fundamental, if hidden, beliefs that we have about the nature of experience.

Imagine someone claiming that there might be a creature whose experience consisted in nothing other than high-level theoretical beliefs about the nature of nuclear interactions – a kind of super-pure physicist. It has nothing that we would call sensory experience, nothing we call desires, and its beliefs are restricted exclusively to this single area of inquiry. In the first place, it is difficult to understand how anything could possess beliefs about a single domain, especially at such an abstract level, without at least the possibility of acquiring beliefs about connected aspects of the world.

Secondly, we think of beliefs as being true or false. But what is it for the super-pure physicist to have true beliefs or false beliefs, if it cannot check its beliefs against experience or even against each other? Further, what does the super-pure physicist do? It just seems to be there, without any immediate causal relation to the world, repeating its beliefs to itself. It must simply 'have' its beliefs. But how is its possession of beliefs to be understood? Well, if we had a full description of the super-pure physicist's 'experience', we would have a set of descriptions of nuclear interactions. But we would have nothing else, since this is *all* there would be to its having experience. In this case, it does not have anything it makes sense to call 'experience'. And now, it seems impossible to think of the super-pure physicist as a creature at all. It is more like a book. And what it has is text.

A general lesson can be drawn from this thought-experiment: do not confuse the notion of an experiencing being with that of a piece of information. The claim that everything is 'really' information – a kind of text – is very common today. It is perhaps the dominant metaphor in contemporary accounts of our understanding of the world. The physical world, it is supposed, must be thought of as information, and so everything that living beings do (themselves composed of information, like other physical things) must be understood as information processing. This means that there must be information which is not information *for* something or someone. This idea is of a piece with the thought we discussed earlier (see pp. 82-3): physical structures embodying representations can be thought of as standing alone, independent of being taken *as* representations.

Now imagine that someone claims there might exist a kind of creature at the opposite extreme from the super-pure physicist. A super-pure sufferer, for example, whose experience consists wholly in the occurrence of extreme pain. There is no connection of the pain with distress nor with perceived threat. It does not engage with a system of preferences. The pain plays no behavioural role in avoidance or flight. When all these connections are severed what is left of 'pain'?

Well, just the awful sensation. But there is nothing which is hurt. But if there is nothing for which the sensation is awful, what makes it 'pain'? Why not call it something else, 'pleasure' for example? The last resort for this thought-experiment might be to suggest that, pain or pleasure, it is in any case a single, all-consuming sensation. But what makes this a 'sensation'? Why not call it an emotion, a perception, a thought? We are asked to deploy our psychological vocabulary in a featureless psychic landscape where we can find no bearings.

Super-pure physicists and sufferers could not survive in the natural world; they could not make a living. But there is more to it than that. They do not make sense; they are not even candidates for inclusion in the natural world. Their impossibility shows that we are already committed to a conception of the kind of thing that experience must be, the properties it cannot do without, the connections it must preserve. Consequently, we cannot deny that an *a priori* conception of experience is possible. We have one.

how wrong might we be?

This conception of experience is *a priori*. It is one that we form in advance of any empirical research into the nature of experience. Still, our *a priori* conception of experience should not be accepted uncritically. It has to be articulated, analysed and assessed and it is vulnerable to both logical and empirical criticism.

How deep could these criticisms go? Might it be that all our thinking about the nature of experience is misconceived at the most fundamental level? Might our deepest, most cherished beliefs about the nature of experience be false?

We suggested in chapter 1 that it is *just* possible that our deepest beliefs about the nature of sentient life are wrong. Perhaps our division of the world into those things that, broadly speaking, are sentient and those things that, broadly speaking, are not sentient, really is a serious misunderstanding of how things actually are. Perhaps whether or not something is sentient, even in the barest, most attenuated sense, is *not at all* the most important question we could ask about it. Maybe, in reality, the fundamental contrast we draw between sentience and non-sentience carves out only a tiny corner of the kinds of way in which it is possible to be something. But it would take more than this bare possibility to persuade us that we were wrong about the fundamental importance of the contrast between the sentient and non-sentient. Nevertheless, maybe we are still in the grip of other systematic illusions about the nature of our experience which would compromise any attempt to think about experience in general.

structure and content

Another radical way in which we might be wrong concerns the distinction between the structure and the content of experience. We distinguish the things we encounter in the world from the world through which they move. In perception we experience objects against backgrounds. We come across things in particular places and at particular times. Places and times form the structured environment within which whatever we encounter in perception comes and goes.

How wrong could we be about this? We might be mistaken concerning the origin of the contrast. Is it a contrast that the external world insists upon or is it based in the physiology of our species? Does our experience consist of objects and the spaces and times through which they move because that is what the world is like? Or, whatever the world was really like, would we be bound, by our biology, to see the world in this way?

We might also be mistaken about the absoluteness of the contrast. Human experimental subjects[1] who are given special spectacles to invert their vision, report that the world appears to be upside-down and, as would be expected, they experience difficulty in finding their way around. After a few days, they report that the world has righted itself, though they now feel that their bodies are upside down. But the most perplexing result of such experiments, is that the subjects report a period of transition, in which the world seems to them neither the right way up nor the wrong way up. Some objects appear to have a normal orientation, whilst others appear odd. Other objects appear to dramatically change their orientation: candles that appear upside down suddenly snap into the correct orientation when lit; cars appear to be driving on the correct side of the road but their licence numbers are reversed. Eventually, objects, the horizon and the subject's body acquire the same orientation, though it remains difficult to locate the direction of sounds. After the experiment, when the spectacles are removed, objects appear the right way up but subjects reach out their right hand when they should reach out their left.

Certainly, the first stage of the experience is startling; to be walking on the ground and still to feel upside down. But the transitionary phase should give us a more profound shock. What, *phenomenally*, is it like to be in this transitionary phase? That is, what is it like as an experience? That the world we experience could lack a definite orientation undermines our confidence in the permanence of the contrast between things and the spaces they occupy. It seems as if, as least sometimes, we can experience objects as carrying their own spatial properties quite independently of whatever else is 'around' them. Here, structure and content seem somehow to interpenetrate. Perhaps human beings are capable, under special conditions, of all kinds of experience in which the apparent absoluteness of the contrast between form and content is undermined.

However, while there is controversy about the details of this contrast and its philosophical implications, this does not mean that we could abandon it. On the contrary, it is precisely in terms of modifications of this contrast that we can understand bizarre and unusual experiences of human beings. But, to admit this is to affirm that we cannot do without the distinction.

Thinking about how wrong we might be about our experience is a route to thinking about the nature of experience different from our own. If, in our experience, the *a priori* contrast between structure and particular things, despite our expectations, can seem to vary, this offers us a way of thinking about the experience of animals very different from ourselves.

picturing animal experience

The contrast between the form and content of experience, when carried over to the non-human world, can, however, tempt us to construct imaginative pictures of animal experience which are too simple. We use these pictures to give content to the idea of animal experience, to define the other end of the spectrum of experience by contrast with our own. In the case of animals whose experience strikes us as being relatively familiar and unproblematic, the models remain in the background. We feel no temptation to picture their inner life. The pictures come to the fore when we are considering animals whose experience must, we feel, be contrasted with our own.

When we reflect upon it, human experience can seem essentially structured. Because of this structure, data is moulded into a determinate and finite range of shapes and sizes. All is neatness, order and intelligibility. So, by contrast, we are tempted to picture an animal mind as the passive recipient of a vast and various array of data, with the animal itself conceived only as an internally feature-less receptacle. The animal mind has only just sufficient structure to make the experiences its own. All is 'an indistinguishable, swarming continuum, devoid of distinction or emphasis'.[2] This picture enables us to think of the animal mind as being 'simpler' than our own; the featureless animal mind is dominated by the content of its experience. We think of the animal as attempting to impose simple structures on a phenomenological pandemonium. We imagine a creature in a constant state of confusion about the world in which it lives.

On the other hand, our experience can seem to be rich in variety, allowing for an indefinite degree of discrimination. All is nuance and novelty. When we are struck by this thought, we picture an animal's experience as impoverished in its content because of its domination by form and structure. At the limit, the animal mind is thought of as dyadic – on/off, light/dark. The simple but enormous structures of the animal mind dominate the content of its experi-ence. We imagine a creature which is in a constant state of ignorance about the world in which it lives.

While these pictures are diametrically opposed they are both attempts to conceive of animal experience as *simpler* than our own. They both involve the thought that animals have less of what we have, either in terms of structure or in terms of content. They draw us in different directions; one towards greater diversity of content, the other towards greater rigidity of structure.

These extreme pictures are produced by our desire for the best of both worlds in our own case. We want to think of our own experience as perfectly ordered *and* indefinitely rich. When we look down on the content of animal experience, what is interpreted as richness in our own case, we see as chaos in theirs. When we look down on the structure of their experience, what is interpreted as active, value-laden and rule-governed in our own case, we see as passive, causal and law-governed in theirs. The effect of the pictures is that we take our experience to be *of* the objective world; their experience to *be* subjective worlds. Our experience reveals how the world is, it is a way of knowing; whereas their experience is just psychological data, only a way of being.

bats and blind-man's-buff

What is naive about these pictures is that they misunderstand the interdependence of content and structure. Bats, for example, use complex systems of echo-location. What must it be like to have this perceptual system?[3] How must it affect the character of the bat's world? When we play blind-man's-buff we use sound clues to find our way around the living room. But certainly we can't believe that bats guess their way around the forest. So how can we describe this difference?

Perhaps what strikes us as odd about echo-location, compared to vision, is that the creature has to do something in order to bring about the perceptual experience; it has to emit, and modulate, the screech. Without the screech, and the reflecting echo, the object is sonically inert. Whereas in order to see something we have only to turn our heads discovering visual properties, which, we feel, were already there. The thought underlying this is that perception in order to count as real perception – as showing, rather than tracking an object – must be passive.

We are familiar, however, with the fact that, in our own case, mastery of 'artificial' means of perception coincides with ceasing to be aware of the artifice. The driver, aware of the icy road, is unaware of the transmission and tyres; the blind man ceases to be aware of the length of his cane. Closer to the bat, the submariner listening on headphones for the enemy ship need pay no attention to the mechanics and electronics of sonar. Turning the dial to redirect the beam comes to seem not a means of doing something to the objects outside the boat, but a way of re-directing one's attention to what is already there, like turning one's head. Because such means of perception are, in our case, artificial and can be contrasted with sight and touch, the feeling persists that this is a kind of illusion, though one to be welcomed and exploited. But this contrast is not possible in the case of bats. Echo-location has to deliver up a world for a bat. The bat cannot take itself as negotiating a world of sonic *experiences*; it experiences a sonic *world*. Hence, what strikes us as the perceptual indirectness, introduced by the need to actively emit modulated sounds, is, from its point of view, no more active and so indirect than our peering or glancing or turning our heads.

This might lead us to think that the difference between the bat and us lies in the kind of objects that the bat's world contains. For those of us who are sighted, objects are constituted by their visual properties, by their colour and shape. For bats, on the other hand, objects are constituted by their sonic properties, by pitch, volume and duration. But can we think of this experience as being just like ours, except that it contains sonic objects in the way that our world contains coloured objects? If this is correct, the bat lives in a world, like ours, except that it contains particular things, which from our point of view are anomalous – objects given as *heard*.

The trouble with this account is that we are thinking of the bat as living in a world which is structured in terms of visual properties while, at the same time, it contains not visual but sonic objects. But it must be clear that there is nowhere in *our* world for the sounded properties of objects to appear in the way that coloured properties of objects appear. What we have to recognise is the extent to which such perceptual systems must *shape the structure* of the bat's world. Echo-location delivers up not a sighted world containing sonic objects, but a sonic world. Sonic qualities determine relative 'location', 'distance', 'size' and so on. Perhaps a better example to feed our imaginations in thinking about bats is our experience of listening to music. We can be acquainted with musical worlds, hear their structures, and, for a time, inhabit the 'spaces' they open up to the ear. The strength of the metaphor is that in music, we do not think that what we hear are merely the perceived qualities of underlying objects to which we might have more direct access. The (musical) object that we experience is constituted by and not merely traceable through the sounds that we hear. The possible structures and content of music are interdependent. Similarly, if echo-location is a creature's dominant mode of perception, what it hears cannot be a clue to the location of an object; it is what it is for the object to be there. But the weakness of the metaphor is also revealing. Our attending to the different parts of the music is not like the bat's being at a different physical location in relation to the sonic objects of its world. The music lover is *imaginatively* moving through an aesthetic world; the bat is *really* moving through a sonic world.

So, thinking about the simplicity of animal experience turns out to be more complicated than it seems at first sight. 'Simplicity' is not simple, because the structure and content of any experience are interdependent – we cannot tinker with one and leave the other untouched. We cannot simply introduce anomalous objects into the worlds of other creatures, which in all other respects resemble ours. If we do, we interpret what is alien, bizarre, different from us, as species-specific noise, something going on in them, something to be swept under the brain, rather than constitutive features of their worlds.

varying the relation between structure and content

When we try to develop an adequately complex picture of experiences different from our own, one thing we can imagine is that the relationship between the structure and the content of a creature's experience may differ from our own. In our case, the structure of our experience is very highly sensitive to the nature of our perceptual and cognitive systems. But non-human animals also differ from us in their repertoire of needs and desires. Appetitive systems too, like perceptual and cognitive systems, may determine the character of the world the animal inhabits.

For us, particular things, like the lunch we eat today, are firmly located at a particular place and time – on the table in front of us, at noon. Most of the time, we take our lives to be passing in a square world, with the cosmic clock ticking reliably in the background. Other places and times have determinate relations to the here and now. But when we attend to our actual experiences, our world is not measured out in fixed increments. Not for everyone will it seem like twenty-four hours to Tulsa. Time seems to pass more or less quickly, stretching and shrinking according to mood, expectations, and present satisfaction.

To imagine experience different from our own is, in part, to imagine more far-reaching changes in these aspects of experience, determined by a creature's fundamental appetites. Its appetites structure the character of the spaces and times accessible to it in more thorough-going ways. Migrating birds must fly south. The urgency they feel is not a function of high-level judgements about the position of the sun, the direction of the wind and changes in temperature. They are not, like us, rushing to catch a train. They do not suddenly remember the time. Still, the urgency of their migration is clear. This behaviour is clearly instinctual; it is produced and controlled by complex causal mechanisms refined through natural selection.

What is it like to have such instincts? If we think that, in general, birds do have experiences, but that there does not have to be an experienced dimension to instinctual behaviour, we may be tempted to think of the bird as being a victim of its unexperenciable instincts. It finds itself flying south. The diametrically opposed view is that there is nothing it is *like* to have the migratory or any other instinct, because there is nothing it is like to be a bird at all. The bird does not find itself flying because it does not find itself anywhere.

Alternatively, we might reject both of these options. The fact that behaviour is instinctual does not mean that it has no character as an experience. After all, some of our own behaviour – for example, sexual behaviour – is instinctual and yet there is certainly something it is like for us to have this behaviour. It may be precisely through experiences that instincts operate. This was the view of George Romanes. If we believe that there is something it is like to be the bird and that the character of its experience is not epiphenomenal, then we need to understand how the character of the bird's experience is shaped by its instincts. We may conclude that the animal experiences migratory desires, or at least that it is anxious and unsettled when the time comes to leave. Which of these possibilities is true is an empirical question that can only be resolved by close observation of the animal and its behaviour. The sort of evidence that would be relevant would be observable changes in mood and behaviour. However, where there is evidence which indicates that the character of experience has a functional significance, how might the experience be conceived? If we assimilate migratory behaviour to human restlessness we may think in terms of annoyance and irritability.

But a less anthropomorphic approach would be to think in terms of structural modification of the creature's world. This was the view of von Uexküll. The considerations we mentioned earlier may now be relevant. Instead of thinking of the migratory birds as aggrieved occupants of an unchanged world, we might think of their temporal world as slewed by the urgency of its imminent migration. The world speeds towards the south.

We cannot, of course, on *a priori* grounds, determine the nature of the migratory experience. The point is only that if we try to make sense of experience very different from our own, we can, and we may have to think more radically about the relationship between what the animal experiences and the temporal backgrounds against which its particular experiences occur.

We also need to think about the spatial aspects of experience. In our human world, perceived spatial qualities are in part determined by what we can do. A room presents itself as a space which gives us choices. Its being a space for us is in part its being an arena for our actions and choices: we can go to the corner of the room and take the papers from the filing cabinet. Our choices may emerge from a simpler pattern of drives, desires and needs than we like to imagine. Still, the way the world presents itself to us spatially is, in part, a function of the choices we are able to make.

Most of us feel more comfortable and secure at home. But the distinctions between what is and what is not our home depend primarily on cultural and contractual practices. Even when there are subliminal clues which play a causal role in our feelings about our own territory, we not do consciously experience our homes as containing such clues. Home and not-home is not a presented perceptual dimension of experience. True, humans are very territorial. The repertoire of our territorial behaviour is realised in numerous ways, institutional and cultural, from estate agencies to world wars. But it leaves the way pieces of ground are actually perceived unaffected. In the human world, even the most important borders are in no way phenomenally remarkable. Hence the need for remarkable signposts.

The lives of other creatures appear to be more tightly bound into the delineation and defence of their territory. Consequently, the character of their sensory experience, and so the shape of their world, may be more thoroughly determined by territorial behaviour. The border between home and non-home may be a *phenomenal* one. The marked and the unmarked territory are not the same bit of world, one with and one without particular odours. At the extreme, the unmarked territory could present itself to the creature as un-navigable, containing no possible object of desire; the marked territory presents itself as intelligible, full of possibilities. Perhaps, when we try to imagine experience different from our own, we have to conceive how food could be experienced as a place to go or how the world might lean away from threats.

Why should the empirical animal researcher take any notice of such considerations? Isn't it all pointless, know-nothing specula-tion? The point of these considerations is not to license unbridled speculation, isolated from any empirical considerations. We have suggested that we cannot ignore the *a priori* conceptions of experi-ence that inform our thinking about our own experience and the experience of others. We have tried to indicate how the content of animal experience cannot be envisaged without at the same time thinking about the possible structures of animal experience and the variable relation between its form and content.

At the very least, thinking explicitly about what it makes sense to say about experience can prevent us from adopting naive pictures of animal experience. It should show us that we cannot imagina-tively tinker with facets of experience without thinking seriously about the effects on the whole of experience and the world in which an animal lives – we do not capture what it is like to have a multi-faceted eye by cutting up and re-pasting segments of photo-graphs we have taken.

the unity of experience

However, even when we try to recognise the role of structural features of experience, we walk into a serious problem. There is a strong philosophical tradition which insists on the need to take seriously the idea of the structure of experience and consequently on the need to give an *holistic* account of experience. Kant, for instance, insisted that the capacity to divide the world into conti-nuing objects is not a capacity which can operate in an otherwise empty conceptual space. To see objects as continuing, I must be able to re-identify objects as being the same objects and this requires a whole set of concepts, including the notion of causal connection. Kant's point was that the fundamental structures of mind and experience must be purchased as a once and for all complete system, not as a starter-kit with optional accessories.

The Wittgensteinian tradition emphasises the complexity of the surroundings that are required for concept application to be possible. Concept possession requires the capacity to follow rules which can be applied correctly or incorrectly. Following rules correctly or incorrectly entails the existence of complex practices and forms of life in which these normative criteria are embedded. So even the use of very simple concepts requires elaborate scaffolding.

Donald Davidson has developed a line of thought which seems to continue the assault on empiricist theories of mind, especially of belief. He stresses how complex the background conditions must be if the foreground empiricist 'atoms' are to be in place. Writing about the human case, Davidson argues that:

> We can...take it for granted that most beliefs are correct. The reason for this is that a belief is identified by its location in a pattern of beliefs; it is the pattern that determines the subject matter of the belief, what the belief is about. Before some object in, or aspect of, the world can become part of the subject matter of a belief (true or false) there must be endless true beliefs about the subject matter. False beliefs tend to undermine the identification of the subject matter; to undermine, therefore, the validity of a description of the belief as being about that subject. And so, in turn, false beliefs, undermine the claim that a connected belief is false.... To put it another way: the more things a believer is right about, the sharper his errors are. Too much mistake simply blurs the focus.[4]

If correct, this implies that the atomistic assumptions of Empiricism are incoherent. A creature could not have one or two beliefs because in such a lunar mental world, there would be no way of fixing their content. They have to exist against the background of patterns of belief, providing mutual determination of content.

Whilst such accounts look perfectly plausible in our case, they may seem to stretch credulity to the limit in the case of other animal minds. The problem is that the structural features of experience cannot be dismantled and transferred piecemeal to the animal kingdom while retaining their formal role. They have to be attributed to animals on an all or nothing basis. The consequence appears to be that the attribution of even a single, simple belief demands that the animal be capable of discriminations and judgements as sophisticated as those which are thought to be necessary for our capacity to have such a belief. Are we really to believe that, whenever an animal experiences any kind of object in the world, it is bringing to bear a whole sophisticated conceptual structure? There just seems to be no room in the life of many of the animals we encounter for such high-grade structural complexity. The worry is that if we give the animal a cognitive inch, then, like the puppy in the Andrex advertisement, it will take a mile.

So, either we apply an account which appears to fit the facts but which there are good reasons to think must be incoherent, or else we adopt the kind of account that we prefer in our case, but which is fundamentally ill-suited to be mapped on to phylogenetic gradation. Our ordinary talk about animals implies that animals do have beliefs and concepts. But, the possession of concepts and beliefs requires a holistic and not an empiricist explanation and we are reluctant to attribute such complexity to other animals. This then is the dilemma facing the philosophical understanding of other animal minds. We seem to face a choice between ascribing more than we want to or withdrawing more than we want to.

We cannot escape the dilemma by pointing out that only humans are linguistic and arguing that holistic accounts are required in the case of linguistic but not in the case of non-linguistic creatures. Our beliefs are expressed in language and our concepts are linguistic concepts. These beliefs and concepts require holistic explanation. But they do so, in virtue of being beliefs and concepts and not in virtue of being linguistic.

Nor can we escape the dilemma by arguing that whereas the holistic story is required for a creature who is aware that it has experiences, it is not required in the case of creatures who have experiences but are not aware that they have them. We cannot escape by saying that 'animals do not see as we do when we are aware that we see, but only as we do when our mind is elsewhere'.[5] The complex background stressed by holistic accounts is presented as something which we need in order to have experience at all and not just to bring experience into reflective awareness. The background is required for us to have beliefs at all, not just to have beliefs about beliefs. Consequently, these holistic considerations do not apply only to self-conscious but also to conscious creatures.

So how, if we accept holism about experience, beliefs and concept-possession, can we make sense of our ordinary talk about animals? At least three demands must be met.

First of all, we must try to understand the structural complexities of the animal's life. We need more than a set of facts about the animals: an endless list of neutral observations. Because animal lives, as well as our lives, are not just one damn thing after another, we need to see what patterns these facts make, how they are connected. Of particular importance in this endeavour is the kind of close attention to, and absorption in the lives, social interactions and expressive repertoire of the animal in its natural habitat, common to the work of contemporary ethologists.

Second, we need to learn to see what is normative in the animal's life. We must understand what in the animal's life corresponds to the following of rules in our own. This does not mean searching for formulated rules that the animal keeps in its head. For, as we saw earlier, it is a mistake to think that this must necessarily be true even in the human case. An animal can be following the rules of pack hunting but not by looking up the rules, making inferences from rules and so on. Rather, the rules are embodied in its social interactions; its myriad acts of co-operation and conflict with its fellows. The Wittgensteinian relocation of concepts from the private mental world to the public social world does not just apply to human concepts. If our concepts are embodied not in something in our heads but in something in our communal life, so too, leonine and wolverine concepts are realised in pride and pack practice.

A challenge for this point of view lies in those creatures who seem to have complex and sophisticated interactions with their environments and yet do not share a communal life with conspecifics. Of course, we need to be careful that we do not wrongly class a creature as non-social. Being non-social is not the same as being solitary. And many relatively solitary creatures have intensely social early lives. While we are more reluctant to attribute anything approaching concept-possession to such creatures, there may yet be something that can function as an analogue of communal life: the species-specific inherited repertoire of expressive behaviour. Imaginative techniques of interaction are needed to see what happens when such creatures do encounter either another creature or something that seems to be like itself.

Learning to see what can count as normative in an animal's life means properly situating ourselves in relation to it. Certainly, we never will see it, if we only ever take an external, objective view; seeing everything that occurs in the life of an animal but understanding nothing of what goes on.

Finally, we need to see how it can make sense to attribute to an animal an open-ended set of beliefs. One reason most of us are happy to say that the dog thinks the cat is up the tree is that the dog could also think, we believe, that the cat is on top of the wardrobe or under the bed. We know that the dog is able to respond to a wide variety of conditions, often in idiosyncratic ways. If we had not lived with dogs and shared our lives with them, if we had only ever seen dogs in laboratories, it is unlikely that we would have these views. Restricting our observations to attenuated 'behaviour' in artificial and controlled environments does not just mean that there are truths about the animal's life that we never discover. It means that the range of things it makes sense for us to say of the creature is severely restricted. In our case, we must treat most of what our fellows believe as true, in order that we can make sense of them at all. Similarly it is only in an environment where we are able to treat the animal's behaviour as relevant, appropriate and viable that the creature's life comes into focus. And only then does the idea of what the individual animal gets right and what it gets wrong, the idea of its having a grip on its world, acquire a sense.

conclusion

In this chapter, we have tried to tackle the question of whether there is anything experience must be. A positive answer to this question means that we have at least a start on understanding the experience of animals different from ourselves. We have seen that, unless we adopt the unattractive position of evolutionary epiphenomenalism, there is some reason to think that there are *a posteriori* limits on experience. But there is also reason to think that *a priori* reflection on the concept of experience is helpful. The insights offered by *a priori* reflection on experience are not necessarily correct. They do need to be moderated by a robust sense of the empirical truth about animal physiology and behaviour. But, on the other hand, we should not allow empirical investigation to ride roughshod over our ordinary views that other creatures do have experiences more or less different from our own.

Two *a priori* insights are of particular importance. First, a creature's experience, if it is to be experience, cannot only be a kind of noise, between it and a world of stimuli. The job of experience is to deliver up a world for the animal. Second, reflection upon the contrast between the structure and content of experience offers one way of thinking about how experience might be different from our own.

However, contemporary *a priori* thinking about the nature of experience also presents a dilemma, one we believe to be fundamental to the problem of understanding animal minds. In the human case, there are good grounds for doubting that an empiricist account of experience, belief and concept possession is tenable. But if holism is required in our own case, why should it not be required in the case of other animals? This dilemma presents a challenge to both contemporary philosophy and the animal sciences. Philosophy, if it is to justify its claims to generality, needs to be far more wary of the risk of species-specificity in its accounts of belief, concept-possession and experience. The animal sciences, for their part, must recognise that objective methodologies alone will not suffice.

There is an important benefit of *a priori* reflection on experience: the attempt to make sense of kinds of experience different from our own, liberates us from the reliance on our own case that bedevils our attempt to think about other animal minds. Maybe we *can* come to see our own experience, not as the inevitable starting and end point of all our thinking about mind, but, for what it is – one possibility among many. Certainly thinking about what experience must be can help us to make the connections required if we are to see the animal in its adaptive, physiological and experential complexity, if we are to understand the *ecology* of experience.

notes

1. This example is discussed in *Molyneux's Question – Vision, Touch and the Philosophy of Perception* by M.J. Morgan (Cambridge University Press, 1977), pp. 171-2. Much discussed in the 17th century, William Molyneux's question concerned whether or not congenitally blind people would, if they regained their sight, be

immediately able to recognise by sight the shapes of objects with which they were familiar through touch.

2. *The Principles of Psychology* by William James (New York, Dover, 1950), vol. 1, p. 284. William James (1842-1910) was an American psychologist and philosopher working at Harvard who wrote extensively on the philosophy of psychology.

3. C.f. 'What is it like to be a bat?', in *Mortal Questions* by Thomas Nagel (Cambridge University Press, 1979).

4. 'Thought and talk' by Donald Davidson in *Inquiries into Truth and Interpretation* (The Clarendon Press, Oxford, 1984), p. 163.

5. Letter to Plempius for Fromondus, René Descartes (October 3, 1637), in *Descartes, Philosophical Letters*, (trans. and ed.) A. Kenny (The Clarendon Press, Oxford, 1970), p. 36. For a fuller discussion of Descartes', views on animal consciousness, c.f. *Descartes, The Project of Pure Enquiry* by Bernard Williams (Harmondsworth, 1978), pp. 278-303.

8: the expressive world

We have now seen something of the philosophical problems and dilemmas that surround the question of animal minds. In this chapter we want to suggest some ways in which we might resolve them.

the alien world

Think for a moment not of animals but of aliens.[1] Imagine intelligent beings who understand the world in ways very different from our own. Our world consists of such things as rivers, cathedrals and financial markets. But ours is not the only possible world. Much of what we take to be the world is constructed by us. It is not, however, a fact peculiar to the human world that it is in part constructed by mind. It is not a consequence of our over-active and powerful imaginations or of any other distinctively human capacity. If *any* animal has a point of view on a world, it must be possible to distinguish between aspects of its experience that are functions of its modes of constructing the world and the world itself. When we imagine aliens with different kinds of experience and different kinds of life we are imagining beings who construct their world differently from the way we do.

In saying this, we do not have to understand what such alien minds would be like. As Kant believed, thinking of different kinds of minds as possible is a way of realising that our experience of the world contains structures which are fundamental and yet contingent. Unless we think that other kinds of minds and correlated worlds are at least possible, even if they are beyond our conception, we are forced to regard our structures as necessary and this will be a mistake. We will be tempted to conflate our way of experiencing the world with how the world really is. An acid test for our views about the reality of anything is whether or not we think that some other concept-using creature must be aware of it, on pain of missing something about how the world really is, independent of its point of view. And so one purpose of imagining alien minds is to test our commitments to what there really is. First of all, however, what must we believe in order to have these commitments at all?

Penalty shoot-outs, choral symphonies and revolutions are certainly not events that exist independently of human thoughts, desires and interests. It would be chauvinist to claim that these ways of carving the stuff of the world are the only ways, or even the best ways of doing it. These concepts, which are dependent on human ways of living, would not appear in the most objective account of the world it is possible for us to give. They do not appear in the 'hard' sciences and we would be surprised if our intelligent alien proved to possess such concepts. We should be disappointed to find that the world and its inhabitants turned out to be so uniform. If we ever meet aliens, we don't wish to discover them playing bingo.

But entertaining the modest proposal that there could be other kinds of minds with correlated worlds does not mean that the concepts we use to structure the human world are globally defective. There is nothing wrong with the concept of a penalty or a choral symphony. Nor does the idea commit us to the extreme thought that *everything* about *our* world is constructed by us. It does not make genuine objective knowledge of reality impossible or even nonsensical, leaving us imprisoned in human subjectivity. On the contrary, we can only take subjectivity seriously if we have a strong sense of objectivity. Part of this commitment to objectivity is the realisation that no beings, not even human beings, are *guaranteed* access to how the world really is. What does matter is that we *can* discover something about what there is independent of our point of view. We must believe that if we work sufficiently hard, we can develop methods, equipment, theories, techniques of calculation and so on which give us a chance of success. So long as we can make this belief stick, our realism is intact and secure.

So, in order to have any commitments to what there really is, we need three interdependent ideas: the humanly constructed world, the world independent of any mind, and the idea of science that takes its origin in the former but arrives at the latter.

To test the actual commitments we have, we need to think about how the intelligent alien's conception of reality might legitimately differ from our own. The alien, with a very different way of thinking and experiencing the world is not to be thought a poor observer simply because it does not describe the world in the way we do. We can hardly fault it because it thinks that the most important thing about the swirl of world that we call a penalty shoot-out is that it contains a high percentage of '*dorns*': a concept picking out a kind of thing very important in *its* life and culture but which is a mystery to us. However, we should hope that, if we could communicate with the alien, we could agree about what really forms part of the objective world. We might agree that there really are such and such particles, these forces, these sorts of structures and so on. Hoping for this is hoping that at least some of our fundamental science is right.

waving at aliens

But maybe we could not communicate. And not simply because we cannot understand each others' language. Perhaps the alien way of looking at the world is so different from ours, that one of the things that they cannot see is *us*. We wave frantically at the passing aliens. But while our movements occur in their world, they do so under quite different descriptions and hence with different kinds of explanation. They treat the stuff making up what we call our bodies as parts of quite different entities in which they have their own interests. What we count as our own actions are taken to be sections of other sequences of events with quite different explanations. They are blind to them *as expressions*. They do not see them as emanating from *us*. They continue their mission, unseeing, unmoved and unresponsive; to boldly catalogue where no one has catalogued before.

Now, the critical question: have the aliens missed something about what there really is in the world?

Of course, we have no problem in imagining creatures who can have no knowledge of us. Many species of animal are in just this position. If lobsters have a world, presumably we are not furniture within it. But we are indifferent to this possibility. It just shows how much of the world the lobster does not or cannot experience.

But, in the case of an intelligent alien who is systematically investigating the real and objective order, we must demand that we be entered into its catalogue of the world. This demand is not motivated merely by self-interest. It manifests our commitment to realism about ourselves in particular and about people in general. Things like us are not inert, as it were, like books in a library waiting to be catalogued according to the convenience of the librarian. We demand a say in the matter. The bottom line is the categorical demand that we be recognised. So, to say that, in describing our waving as some quite different sequence of events, the aliens have not missed anything at all is to say that we, as particular people are not *real*. This carries self-abnegation to vertiginous heights. However accommodating we try to be about different perspectives on the world, we cannot tolerate our own omission from the world.

What the aliens failed to do was recognise that we were waving at them. And however they divide the world up, they should not miss *that*. This is to miss something about how the world really is – that we are in it. Their ontology – the sorts of things that they believe are real – is impoverished. And its poverty is caused by their blindness to our waving, to our expressions.

Expressive behaviour is at the centre of any misunderstanding between us and the aliens because expression is the way in which subjective points of view show themselves in the world. Automata can have behaviour, at least in the accepted, though perhaps corrupted, sense of that term. But nothing can make an automaton's behaviour *expressive* behaviour. Precisely because expressive behaviour does manifest a point of view in the world it cannot be re-described at the convenience of anyone who happens to pass by as simply this or that sequence of events or movements. Because expression manifests a point of view, the truth about it is independent of points of view.

Are we in this position in relation to non-human animals? Do we miss what is really going on in animal worlds? Perhaps, as a matter of fact, our relation to some animals is the same as that of the aliens to us. We may find it difficult to understand the significance of a particular creature's behaviour. Or we may even find it problematic to see anything some creatures do as forming a coherent sequence of behavioural moves; we don't see where one behavioural sequence ends and another begins. Or we find it difficult to see what the creature does as behaviour at all. Nothing the creature does seems to emanate from a point of view on the world. Still, even if the creature does not 'wave' at us, we might suspect that we are missing something about what there is in the world. To discover the truth, to close the gap between the animal's world and ours, it would

be natural to look to the animal sciences.

But, according to a dominant strand of thought in the animal sciences, there is no gap to close. We do not stand to non-human animals as the aliens stand to us. When we do not include animal minds in our stock-taking of the sentient world, nothing real has been left out. One task of the animal sciences is to remind us that we are not mistaken in our stock-taking. Despite the powerful temptations to think otherwise, no one is waving, to us or to anything else.

The point of the story of the alien is to identify just what part of the world it is that they miss if they do not recognise the reality of our point of view. They fail to see us waving. But it also identifies the kind of thing *we* are missing when we deny that other animals could have points of view. The pieces of world that we miss, or misdescribe, are those objects and events which, as a matter of fact, make up a creature's *expressive behaviour*.

If we are really to get to grips with the problem of animal minds then we must understand the key role of expression, not only in recognising other minds, but in the very idea of another mind. It is therefore to the structures of the expressive life that we now turn.

expression in general

There is a difference between telling somebody about something and expressing something to somebody. This is not a merely semantic point: 'Expression' is a portmanteau word, it can refer to any type of utterance, any sort of speaking out, including 'expressions' of opinion. But it has a more specific sense. We talk of 'expressions of feeling', or of 'expressing oneself'. In these senses there is a suggestion of disclosure, of revealing something about oneself or of sharing one's experience. It implies a directness of communication between one person and another which is not involved in descriptions or reports even of one's subjective experience. There is much more going on in such transactions than we might think if our only model of personal communication is the storing and transmission of information.

There is a complex structure even to the most everyday exchanges, whenever people laugh together, insult each other, invite each other for a drink, when one person acknowledges another person in any way. Typical examples of expression in this sense of direct personal communication would be: Norm spoke irritably to

Norma; Norm is sulking because he did not get his own way; Norm and Norma clung on to each other in fear.

The shape of this structure can be detected by putting a series of questions to an instance of expression: who, with what, expressed what, about what, to whom and in what context? These six questions (see below) bring out relevant features of expression:

A Who?	Norm	**Agent**
B With what?	Voice	**Medium**
C What?	Nostalgia	**Content**
D About what?	Tyneside	**Intentional object**
E To whom?	Norma	**Receptor**
F In what context?	In the bar at the Free Trade Inn	**Context**

The above represents the situation in which Norm expresses to Norma his nostalgia for Tyneside by singing *The Blaydon Races* in the bar at the Free Trade Inn. These elements fall into four groups which are features of expression in general.

- A implies *agency*.
- B implies *embodiment*.
- C and D imply *determinacy of sense*.
- E and F imply a *community of expression*.

What we want to suggest is that whether animals have *minds* can be understood as a set of questions about whether the lives of animals exhibit these characteristics of expression. And the further question, *can we understand* anything about animal minds depends on whether we can position ourselves in such a way that these features of expression become visible to us. In what follows, we shall try to make these ideas more precise.

expression and agency

Expression is a type of action. We attribute many aesthetic qualities to natural sounds and movements but there are numerous qualities that apply only to expressive behaviour because they imply agency: repressed, unrestrained, uncertain, tentative, bombastic, forced, spontaneous, hysterical, controlled.

This immediately raises a fundamental problem. To take seriously the expressions of animals and our interactions with them is to attribute agency to animals; and if agency, the nightmare continues, freedom; and if freedom, the end of the determinist model of animal behaviour without which it cannot be susceptible to scientific investigation. This is close to the heart of the opposition to participative methodologies in animal studies and of the advocacy of an exclusively objective approach. The attribution of agency to non-humans must be the worst extravagance of anthropomorphic thinking and the end of scientific understanding.

Agency is seen as an obstacle to scientific understanding because it is thought of as outside the natural order. For this reason, the rejection of non-objective methodologies is often inspired by a clandestine Dualism of determined system and 'free will'. If the clandestine dualist, like the overt dualist of the past, wishes to separate human beings from the natural order, he may welcome the idea that human agency is exempt from scientific scrutiny. If, however, he looks forward to the day when human behaviour will be scientifically explicable like any other natural phenomena, he may merely tolerate the human exemption on a temporary basis. But in either case there can be no exemption for brute animals who are already fully paid up members of the natural order. For the clandestine dualist, we cannot allow agency to animals without applying to them full citizenship and the moral standing of a Kantian autonomous agent. We ought to hang wolves for sheep-stealing and we ought never to use them as means to an end, human or otherwise.

Our intuitive attitude to animals, on the other hand, assumes that there is no dichotomy between human agency and animal behaviour. We do not make a single absolute distinction between the dynamisms of animal life and the 'will' we attribute to ourselves. As Aristotle[2] pointed out, we apply the distinction between voluntary and involuntary to animal action as well as to human action.

He captured the common sense commitment when he categorised animals, the animate, as self-movers. We apply a large range of voluntaristic vocabulary to the behaviour of some animals. They can be frustrated, persistent, unwilling, hesitant, even steadfast and patient.

A test of whether we have really rejected Dualism in our philosophical hearts is whether we are prepared to see agency as a concept that allows of degrees and as a reality which has evolved from the appetitive life of the animal kingdom. A benefit of concentrating on expressive behaviour is that it serves to undermine the glib dualist contrast between active, wilful behaviour and passive will-less bodily events. Too often we think of human actions as the outcome of deliberate processes of cognition and calculation issuing finally in a moment of decision, in which we move our bodies to act. When we are sceptical about the presence of such high level cognitive capacities in animals we are tempted to conclude that everything which an animal body does is a matter of something happening to it.

Expression, however, though it is action, is not easily describable as either active or passive. Someone tells a joke and we laugh. We can be helpless with laughter or we can laugh out of a sense of social politeness. We are sensitive, perhaps hyper-sensitive to the embarrassed laugh, the forced laugh, the nervous laugh. Laughter allows of a whole range of degrees of control, helplessness, spontaneity and contrivance. But in most cases we are at a loss to say whether our response is involuntary or chosen. The distinction between spontaneous and forced, which does apply to expressions, runs parallel to the active/passive distinction, but is very different. It refers to the pressures and compulsions of social interactions which are different from the causes and outcomes of physical processes. Laughing because the joke is funny is not describable in terms of a stark contrast between autonomous action and determined behaviour.

Still, one way in which it becomes clear that expressions are actions of agents is that they can be modulated. We teach children to control their expressions of frustration or anger and even of distress. This training involves a moulding of their inner lives; it is not merely an attempt to keep the peace in the playground or supermarket. There is a close connection between the nature and intensity of feelings and the way we express them. Cries can be loud

just another *epistemological* concept – one more reason for thinking that the concept of knowledge must dominate our thinking about mind and world. This insistence on seeing the whole issue of animal minds as a problem of knowledge, as a matter of what we can and cannot know, continues to lead many to deny that interactive methodologies in the animal sciences can be genuinely scientific. We now need to address this issue.

The reluctance to accept interactive methodologies as genuinely scientific depends on insisting that knowledge, if it is to be scientific knowledge, must be both objective and empirical. Interactive methodologies are not objective – the insights garnered come through, and not in abstraction, from the researchers' perspective. Nor are they thought to be empirical, at least not in the sense that they are based upon reproducible experiment. Interactions between humans and say, great apes, may be sustained and they may be recorded but they are unlikely to be exactly reproducible. Hence, interactive methodologies, whatever else they are, cannot produce knowledge worthy to be called scientific.

This sceptical conclusion results from failing to get right the delicate balance between, on the one hand, the need to avoid over-abstraction from our own point of view and, on the other, the need to avoid over-reliance on our own case.

abstracting from points of view

It is right that someone engaged in scientific inquiry should require an empirical base for their knowledge, acquired in a way that is free from bias and which results in information sharable with others. But the pressure to produce knowledge which has these characteristics can lead and, we believe, in the animal sciences, has led to the false identification of empirical methodology with the push for objectivity. Knowledge can be gathered objectively and it can be gathered empirically. But it is a mistake to think that these are just the same.

Objectivity is primarily a method of understanding.[1] The point of being objective is to ensure the truth of what we discover by eliminating all relevant biases. When we gather knowledge using objective methods, we try, as far as possible, to abstract from our own individual perspective, from our own social and cultural dispositions, from human ways of experiencing the world and, at the limit, perhaps in pure mathematical descriptions of the world, even from the idea of a point of view at all. But this limit is not an ideal which we should always be striving for. Objectivity is a matter of degree – we need to be more or less objective, depending on the nature of the biases which may prevent us from discovering the truth. Where we do need to be objective to some degree, abstracting from our own personal idiosyncrasies, it does not follow that the more objective we are the better. Striving to reach the limit of objectivity may be not just unnecessary to a particular project of enquiry, it may be inimical to it. We do not arrive at more objective views of our careers or our families by trying to describe them mathematically. Sociologists and psychologists aim for objective knowledge of, say, human social and mental disorders. But this does not mean that they must describe their subjects in the language of physics. If they do, they will no longer be engaged in the social and psychological sciences. Outside physics at least, one does not eliminate relevant biases in one's point of view, by seeking to eliminate the very idea of a point of view. So, objective knowledge is not, despite the view of some, simply synonymous with certain knowledge or with respectable knowledge or even with scientific knowledge.

Nor can objective knowledge mean the same as empirical knowledge. To gather knowledge empirically is to use our experience of the world, rather than abstract reasoning alone. The kind of experience involved may itself be highly attenuated. It may mean noting the blips on a computer screen. In physics, empirical knowledge may be highly objective knowledge. But most of our knowledge of the world, and of each other, is empirical without being objective in the way that physics is objective. So, it is quite possible to come to know things empirically yet not abstract entirely from our own point of view. It does not follow that such knowledge must in some way be suspect, biased, unreproducible. Equally, that some knowledge is objective does not mean that it was arrived at through observation and experiment. Mathematical knowledge is objective knowledge but it is not empirical.

'Empirical knowledge' gets the sense it has by contrast with the idea of knowledge derived from reasoning alone. Suspicion about the possibility of such *a priori* knowledge has led to the term 'empirical' being used to mean genuine knowledge. But, as we saw in chapter 7, *a priori* reasoning is not something that we can do without. Knowledge always requires data and processing; data without processing is an unintelligible jumble; processing without data is empty.[2] Especially where different kinds of knowledge need to be synthesised into an overall understanding of a complex reality, conceptual questions are never far away. This means that non-empirical objective knowledge also has a role. Thinking about the nature of psychological concepts, reasoning about the limits, if any, on the concept of experience that we employ, is not a kind of armchair version of these other kinds of knowledge. It is (armchair) thought.

So, the objection to interactive methodologies depends upon a misunderstanding of the relation between the objective and the empirical. Such methods can be objective enough, that is free from relevant bias, and yet they need not involve deliberately forsaking the stance from which the expressive capacities of animals are evident. The fundamental obligation for a scientist, however, is to use those methods which will yield genuine and reliable knowledge. There are in the animal sciences diverse methods which yield knowledge. So we should use them. In order for the animal sciences to use all the different kinds of knowledge available what matters is that we situate ourselves in the proper relation to the object of enquiry – what we have to get right is our relation to animals.

Science has seemed to many to involve giving up the idea, central to Gnosticism, that there is a special place from which alone truths about the world are visible. Interactive methodologies seem to threaten (and ought to threaten) this scientific renunciation. If successful, they imply that there *are* aspects of the world which are only available from particular, partial perspectives. We believe that the animal sciences should learn to live with the fact that participation in the world, and not only disengagement from it, can be a route to knowledge.

relying on our point of view

But there is something else which may prevent us from being in the right place in relation to animals. If interactive methodologies are possible in the animal sciences we need to understand why they work. We must get away from the idea that what we can understand about other animals must always depend on what we understand about our own case; that we make progress only by extended analogical arguments.

Interactive methodologies do not function because the ethologist is an agile analogist; the scientist in the field, working with animals, does not need to be constantly making comparisons between her behaviour and her experience on the one hand, and on the other, the behaviour of the animals and by inference the character of their experience. Interactive methodologies work because there are overlapping similarities between the life of a human ethologist and the lives of at least some other creatures that she studies. That is, what we need to see is that there is a difference between these two statements:

   a) Animal pain is like ours.
   b) Like us, animals experience pain.

The first statement is analogical. If we think that statements of this kind are the foundation of all our thinking about animals we are saying that we must always be engaged in the analogical modelling of the subjective qualities of their experience on the subjective qualities of our own. All our thought and talk about animal minds is an exercise in *comparative objective phenomenology*. It is phenomenology because it aims to capture the subjective qualities of experience; it is *objective* phenomenology because it aims to establish the nature of these experiences, as they are in themselves; it is *comparative* objective phenomenology because its methods of arriving at the knowledge to which it aspires are based on a comparison with our own experience. Where else, we say, can we start but from our own experience?

But when the dog greets its master returning from work or the chick recognises its parent returning to the colony, we do not understand what occurs in these exchanges by first thinking of human communications and drawing an analogy between our own greetings and these others. This is what is expressed by statements of the kind 'Animal pain is like ours'. But we are not engaged in a series of particular analogies between our behaviour and the behaviour of other animals on the one hand, and, on the other, our experiences and the experiences of other animals.

In the human case, I know that you are angry and how angry you are, not because of an analogy between your behaviour and mine, but because we share a common life of which anger and other emotional responses are dimensions. So, too, in the animal case. The shape of the animal's life shows us the kinds of things it can contain. If there is a comparative element in our thinking it involves large-scale comparisons between our lives and the lives of other species. For example, in our lives and in the lives of dogs and penguins (though perhaps not in the lives of sea anemones) there is room for greeting. 'Like us, animals experience pain', that is, our lives share common shapes. In tracing this shape, evolutionary theory, animal physiology, psychology, comparative psychology, zoology, ecology, behavioural studies, cognitive ethology and conceptual analysis all have vital parts to play. Neo-behaviourist approaches, interactive ethology and the metaphysics of experience are all different but complementary means of coming to understand animal minds. (See Fig. 9.1.)

the octopus

Octopuses are members of the family Octopodinidae, which consists of three genera – *Eledone*, *Haplochlaena* and *Octopus*.[3] While they are cephalopods, a branch of molluscs, like vertebrates, they have large and centralised brains, closed circulatory systems and a sophisticated sensory apparatus including great visual acuity and chemotactile means of finding prey. They have an elaborate but mysterious expressive repertoire of colour changes. They are also able to inflict highly toxic bites. The tiny young of most species, less than pea-sized at birth, are not tended by kin and spend months floating like plankton before descending to the sea-bottom. Their lives which range from the six months of *Octopus joubini* to the four years of *O. dofleini*, are mostly spent alone.

Researchers report a range of problems with investigating octopuses in captivity. First of all, octopuses regularly escape from their aquaria. These escapes involve great strength but also great ingenuity though they usually result in death due to lack of oxygen. Their strength enables them to lift heavy tank lids – two octopuses with body weights of only 480 and 350 grams escaped from tanks whose lids were secured by bricks weighing 19.8 kilograms. Their soft-bodies enable them to pass through extremely small gaps and holes. One octopus held in a Brighton aquarium spent most nights climbing into a neighbouring tank to feed on lumpfish and then returning to its own tank. Another held in a tank with an undergravel filter made from egg-crates held together with glue, strong nylon mesh and cable, in one night had 'removed the gravel from the corners, broken the egg crate, torn up the nylon screen and cut through the nylon cable'.[4] In other cases, researchers carrying out

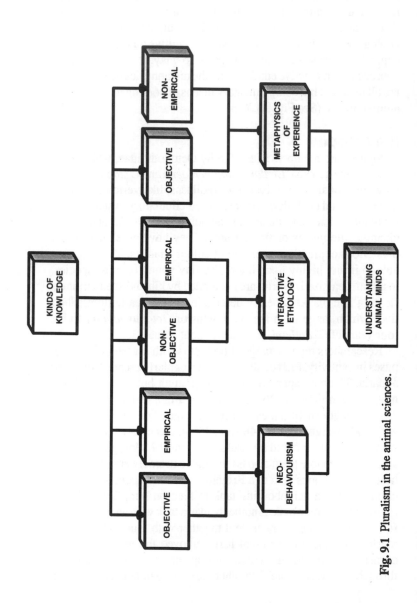

Fig. 9.1 Pluralism in the animal sciences.

a standard stimulus–response test involving the pulling of levers were disrupted by the subject's destruction of the test machinery.

Further, many octopuses shoot jets of water at individual researchers, and seem able to distinguish between individuals who have upset them and individuals who are new to the lab. An octopus prepared for neurophysiological investigation ruined the experiment by pulling out the probes. The response of the investigator was to cut off the creature's arms. The counter-response of the octopus was to shoot a jet of water at the recording apparatus, shorting out the equipment.

Finally, the behaviour in captivity of individual octopuses is highly unpredictable. One type, *O. rubescens*, which has been investigated for individual differences shows very large variation in response to a set of standard stimuli such as opening the lid of the tank.

What is significant about the animal sciences' investigation of octopuses is not that they do not recognise that these are remarkable and, in many ways, very complex creatures. It is that they continue to investigate them using standard stimulus–response methods which are clearly inadequate to the task of understanding them. As the animal scientist Jennifer Mather points out, not only must 'future research on octopuses...be designed to cope with the problems of interaction between researcher and subject',[5] these interactions are themselves the key to understanding their lives and minds. The octopus should be seen as a symbol of our failure to take the diversity of mind seriously.

can we understand animal minds?

So can we, in the end, understand animal minds? The answer is *yes, we can*. But only if we are prepared to jettison the dogmas of the past which so narrowed the concept of what understanding animal minds could mean. When we lose these prejudices, there is all the evidence in the world for the mindfulness of the natural world. Everything in our ordinary and extraordinary encounters with animals speaks for it. We have argued in this book that we can come to understand the natural, mindful world, in all its diversity, but only if we open our philosophical minds to a much more pluralistic concept of knowledge than has hitherto been allowed.

Still, philosophy only clears the undergrowth from the path – though it is a task that needs continuous attention. Progress in understanding the nature of the minds with which we share the world will depend on *scientific* innovation and ingenuity and persistence. Once we have liberated ourselves from philosophical mysteries about 'knowledge of animal minds', we need no longer treat other animals as soft machines nor as strangely silent persons; we can continue the difficult empirical enterprise of getting to know them as animals.

notes

1. *The View From Nowhere* by Thomas Nagel (Oxford University Press, 1986), p. 4.

2. *Critique of Pure Reason* by Immanuel Kant (MacMillan, London, 1929) B75/A51.

3. Cited and discussed in 'Understanding the octopus' by Jennifer Mather, in *The Inevitable Bond – Examining Scientist–Animal Interactions*, (eds) Hank Davies and Dianne Balfour (Cambridge University Press, 1992), pp. 240-9. This book is a fascinating anthology of scientists' accounts of their relationships with other animals in the course of their research.

4. *The Inevitable Bond – Examining Scientist–Animal Interactions*, p. 243.

5. *The Inevitable Bond – Examining Scientist–Animal Interactions*, p. 248.

index of names

can't we make moral judgements? by Mary Midgley

How many times do we hear the statement, 'It's not for me to judge'? It conveys one of the most popular ideas of our time: that to make judgements of others is essentially wrong. But doesn't this idea itself involve a moral judgement? What is it? Could we possibly avoid making it? Why have so many thinkers urged us to do this impossible thing?

In this lively and approachable discussion, Mary Midgley turns a spotlight on the fashionable view that we no longer need or use moral judgements. Guiding the reader through the diverse approaches to this complex subject, she points out the strong, confident beliefs about such things as the value of freedom that underlie our supposed scepticism about values. She shows how the question of whether or not we can make moral judgements must inevitably affect our attitudes not only to the law and its institutions, but also to events that occur in our daily lives, and suggests that mistrust of moral judgement may be making life even harder for us than it would be otherwise.

does God exist? by Mark Corner

Do people talking about God know what they are talking about? Are they all talking about the same thing? How do different religions approach the existence of God? Can God's existence be proved? And even if it can, is God necessarily good?

Does God Exist? sets out to provide a lively and readable introduction to the main issues of theism and atheism. With careful avoidance of theological jargon, the author takes a fresh look at the question that has always been at the very roots of philosophy.

mad or bad? by Michael Bavidge

Michael Bavidge's question, 'Mad or Bad?' arises out of a long-standing philosophical interest in the connections between ethics and the philosophy of mind and from surprise at the verdicts in some notorious murder trials.

Dreadful crimes demand total, unreserved condemnation and heavy punishment, but their very dreadfulness also leads us to think, 'Anyone who does *that* must be nuts?'

This book provides a thought-provoking and sensitive new attempt to show us how we can preserve our ordinary moral intuitions about dreadful crimes while facing up to the difficulties of holding psychopathic criminals fully responsible for their actions. It is an important topic with wide-ranging implications which affect us all.

do we have free will? by Mark Thornton

'Do We Have Free Will' is not just an abstract philosophical question, because our answer to it has enormous influence in many areas of our lives. It shapes educational and legal theory, it underlies particular views in Sociology and Psychology, and it is apparent in decisions in social and political policy.

Mark Thornton has produced an elegant and comprehensive guide to the rich variety of philosophical opinion on the subject. His clear exposition, penetrating criticism and original suggestions make this a valuable book for anyone with a practical or a theoretical concern with issues of human freedom and responsibility.

minds, brains and machines by Geoffrey Brown

Whether or not machines can think is the stuff of which dreams and nightmares are made. Geoffrey Brown lives in this world, however, and his expertise in computing engineering gives him a down-to-earh view of the present complexity and future possibilities of the machines which appear to control much of our lives.

But he is also a philosopher who sees that the question demands careful consideration of some fundamental issues. What do we mean by 'think'? Is machine 'thinking' like human 'thinking'? What does it mean to be conscious? And in answering these questions we reach the heart of what is called the philosophy of mind.

reasonable care by Grant Gillett

If any discipline poses questions of life and death it is medical ethics. Where the availability of treatment is limited, who should get priority? Should doctors force treatment of unwilling patients? How can we judge whether a life is worth living, and who should decide?

Reasonable Care helps us approach these questions by offering a survey and critique of contemporary medical ethics, but it does so by drawing heavily on actual practice and the problems faced by doctors, nurses and their patients.

Grant Gillett is ideally placed to straddle the philosophical and the practical worlds, because when he is not writing and teaching philosophy he spends his time doing neurosurgery.